# Indian Christianity

# Indian Christianity

## An Alternate Reading

**Roger E. Hedlund**

Clark Centre for Peace Research and Action (CCPRA)
**Clark Theological College**
&
**Christian World Imprints™**

CCPRA Publication Series No. 6

First Published in 2016 by

Clark Centre for Peace Research and Action (CCPRA)
**Clark Theological College**
Aolijen, Mokokchung 798601 / Nagaland
ctcprin@gmail.com
www.ctcnagaland.com
Phone: 09436006979

&

**Christian World Imprints**(TM)
*Christian Publishing & Books from India*
H-12 Bali Nagar, New Delhi-110015
info@christianworldimprints.com
www.ChristianWorldImprints.com
Phone: +91 11 25465925

ISBN: 978-93-5148-121-8 (HB)
ISBN: 978-93-5148-122-5 (PB)



Printed at Replika Press Pvt. Ltd.

# Foreword-1

As a former student of Dr. Hedlund, I am very happy to know that in his honour, Clark Theological College is publishing his book on Indian Christianity in recognition of his contribution to the Indian church. It is happening at a time when friends and family members of Dr. Hedlund had just recently celebrated his 80$^{th}$ birthday and that *Dharma Deepika*, a journal which he managed in Chennai, has completed 20 years of its publication. For me, this is the 40th year of my association with Dr. Hedlund, who has remained a teacher and a friend to me upto this day. For this reason, I thought I should introduce Dr. Hedlund as a teacher, writer and organiser; and his work here in India in some detail in this write-up.

Dr. Roger Hedlund, the youngest of his four siblings, was born in the remote north-western corner of Minnesota, USA. In 1961, he married Thea June List. They have two chidren, Karl and Lisa; seven grandchildren; and four great-grandchildren. After his theological studies at Denver, the Hedlunds applied to CBFMS (now WorldVenture) and were appointed to Italy where they served for a term. Later they moved to Naples making the town of Aversa their home where they worked as church planters for one term. Returning to USA, he did further study in missiology at Fuller Seminary with a view to teach. He was an M.A and D.Miss. at Fuller Theological Seminary in 1974 and later a Ph.D. from the University of Madras in 2004. During a break from doctoral studies at Fuller, a four-month teaching opportunity at Discipleship Training Centre in Singapore gave him exposure to the enticing world of Asia. Thus, in 1974 his family relocated in India in response to the two-year invitation to teach Missiology, by Dr. Saphir Athyal, the then Principal of the Union Biblical Seminary at Yavatmal (now at Pune).

## Union Biblical Seminary (UBS), Yavatmal

From 1974 to 1978 he served fulltime at UBS. During this time, I met the Hedlunds in Yavatmal. I was studying B.D. at Union Biblical Seminary during those years. From my encounters with Dr. Hedlund, I came to know that as much as he had come to teach, he was also prepared to learn from India. Our meetings for my thesis writing was an enriching and enabling experience for both of us.

While at UBS, Yavatmal, he was confronted with the need for missiological study materials. Textbooks were not readily available in those days. His class notes, which were mimeographed with the help of June Hedlund, his wife, served as study material for 'The Mission of the Church', a prescribed Serampore syllabus course. These notes were revised and published later as a book with the title, *Mission to Man in the Bible*, published at Madras. A later incarnation by Baker Books (Grand Rapids, USA) preserved the entire text under the more salubrious title, *The Mission of the Church in the World, A Biblical Theology*. Much later ISPCK, Delhi, requested a "contextualized" version, leading to revision and a third incarnation as *God and the Nations, A Biblical Theology of Mission in the Asian Context*, which is now in its second edition. Another UBS course, 'Contemporary Trends in Mission', which went through a similar process of recording and transcription, became a source book consisting of the class lectures and supporting documents from major mission conferences of the Twentieth Century. This was published in 1981 as *Roots of the Great Debate in Mission*. A revised edition was published in 1993 by TBT in Bangalore and reprinted in 1997.

Mission subjects at UBS were popular--an indication of mission enthusiasm in the student body. This had several expressions. Students initiated their first student-led mission conference in 1977. This was to become an annual event.

## Church Growth Centre, Madras

After leaving UBS, his research and writing projects continued through the Church Growth Research Centre at Madras along with seminars, conferences and 'McGavran Institute' courses at various locations throughout India. Before coming to India, Dr. Donald McGavran, Dean of the School of World Mission at Fuller Seminary, encouraged Dr. Hedlund "to get to know the Indian church."

At a conference of the Evangelical Fellowship of India in Devlali, he met church leaders who felt that India should have its own Church Growth Centre. This led to the formation of a committee consisting of seven members; three major consultations with Dr. Donald McGavran and Dr. Virgil Gerber in Bombay, Calcutta, and Madras; and concluding with a National Consultation at Hyderabad in August 1978. "Faith projections" by the participants of these seminars called for establishment of 661 new churches in the next five years. Thus, the Church Growth Association was formed, and Dr. Hedlund served as an Acting Director.

The three aims of the Church Growth Research Center (CGRC) were Research, Publishing, and Training. The Publishing and Training wings developed first. The *India Church Growth Quarterly* (ICGQ) began in 1978. With a heightened awareness of what God was doing among the nations, CGRC produced several books, *Evangelization and Church Growth Issues from the Asian Context* (1992), *Building the Church* (1982), *Roots of the Great Debate* (1981), *Many Other Names? Questions of Religious Pluralism* (ca 1992); and also various other articles and papers. A significant contribution of CGRC was the translation, distribution and use of Vergil Gerber's 1973, *Manual for Evangelism/Church Growth,* which was utilized in church growth seminars in several Indian languages.

Research was the last wing of the organization to develop when Michael and Dawna Jaffarian came specifically to help gather data for analyzing the steady growth of the Madras Churches. The *Madras Churches Directory* was published in 1981, and in 1984 Mr. Vasantharaj Albert became the first Indian Director of it.

In 1986, The McGavran Institute was started in their home in Anna Nagar, and Church Growth Training Seminars were held all across India – North to South, East to West, from Kashmir to Kerala and from Andhra Pradesh to Gujarat. The impact of the Church Growth Research Centre is still felt in several countries around the world.

After leaving CGRC, he continued teaching from time to time at UBS, YCLT, COTR, SAIACS, and Serampore; and also travelled to Sri Lanka, Pakistan, Bangladesh, Nepal, Korea, Philippines, Japan and the U.K. to give lectures.

## Serampore College

In 1994, Hedlund was invited to Serampore College as Professor of Mission Studies/ Research where he served for three years. At Serampore, he encountered something of the classical Bengali culture as well as the Carey tradition. He was put in charge of the Carey Library. This proved beneficial for research leading to an eventual Ph.D. in Christian Studies at the University of Madras. Before arriving at Serampore, however, several persons had been discussing the possibility of creating an academic missiological journal for Christian apologetic and dialogue in the Hindu world context. At a meeting in Hyderabad in 1994, it was put forth by George David, C.V. Mathew, J.C. Gamaliel, Viju Abraham to launch a new journal of missiological research. Hence, *Dharma Deepika: A South Asian Journal of Missiological Research* came into being as a 100-page semi-annual periodical with C.V. Mathew as its editor, and Hedlund as managing editor. Serampore proved fertile ground for ideas, writers and reviewers of this new journal. The purpose was to stimulate creative thinking and encourage scholarly writing.

## Churches of Indigenous Origin

Indian expressions of Christianity had always fascinated Hedlund. Opportunity for research in this area came while he was in Serampore. He and his colleague, O. L. Snaitang applied to the OMSC Research Enablement Programme for a post-doctoral book-writing grant to study Churches of Indigenous Origins in India (CIO). Instead of one book, they produced three: *Quest for Identity: India's Churches of Indigenous Origin*, authored by me; an edited collection with the title, *Christianity Is Indian: The Emergence of an Indigenous Community*; and *Churches of Indigenous Origins in North East India* , edited by O. L. Snaitang. All three were published in 2000 by ISPCK on behalf of the Mylapore Institute for Indigenous Studies (MIIS). A fourth title in the Indigenous Christianity series was published in 2003, *The New Wine-Skins: The Story of the Indigenous Missions in Coastal Andhra Pradesh, India* by the well-known Christian artist and scholar, the Rev. Dr. P. Solomon Raj. Other titles published by ISPCK for MIIS include *A German Exploration of Indian Society, Ziegenbalg's "Malabarian Heathenism": An annotated English translation with an introduction and a glossary* by Daniel Jeyaraj (2006); *Missiology for the 21st Century: South Asian Perspectives* edited by R. E. Hedlund and Paul Joshua Bhakiaraj (2004); *Indian & Christian: The Life and Legacy of Pandita Ramabai* edited by R. E. Hedlund, Sebastian Kim and Rajkumar Boaz Johnson (2011), as well as others.

## Mylapore Institute for Indigenous Studies (MIIS)

At present, Dr. Hedlund is the Director of the MIIS, which is a direct outgrowth of the CIO project, to initiate the study of Indigenous Christianity as a field for academic research in Indian universities and colleges. In addition to the books mentioned above, a spate of academic papers and presentations and essays appeared in several journals and collections. His vision is for MIIS to build upon this. The goal should be the creation of a documentation centre for New Christian Movements in South Asia. A start was made in collecting publications of some of the Independent churches and movements. Later on, this will include documents, photographs, artifacts, recordings, etc. A model for this can be seen in the work of Andrew Walls in Africa, the Centre for the Study of Non-Western Christianity at Aberdeen and at Edinburgh, as well as the Andrew Walls Centre for the Study of African and Asian Christianity.

## Dr. Hedlund as a Writer

Apart from his role as a teacher and a church planter, Dr. Hedlund has written extensively on Missions. He has authored several books and also edited a number of volumes. He has also contributed many Essays which are published in Collections; and contributed a number of articles in Theological Journals.

*Books Authored:*

- *Quest for Identity: Indian Churches of Indigenous Origin, The 'Little Tradition' in Indian Christianity*. Delhi, MIIS & ISPCK, 2000.
- *God and the Nations: A Biblical Theology of Mission in the Asian Context*. Delhi, ISPCK, 1998, 2002.
- *The Mission of the Church in the World, A Biblical Theology*. Grand Rapids, MI, Baker Book House, 1991. (Korean translation 1991; 2nd Indian ed. 1994; Russian translation 1998).
- *Evangelization & Church Growth Issues from the Asian Context*. Madras, CGRC, 1992.
- *Mission to Man in the Bible*. Madras, ELS, 1985.
- *Building the Church*. Madras, CGRC, 1982.
- *Roots of the Great Debate in Mission*. Madras 1981. Revised 1993, TBT, Bangalore. Third ed. reprint 1997.
- *The Protestant Movement in Italy*. Pasadena, WCL, 1970.

*Books Edited:*

- *Oxford Encyclopaedia of South Asian Christianity*, with Jesudas M. Athyal, Joshua Kalapati & Jessica Richard. New Delhi, OUP, 2012.
- *Indian & Christian: The Life and Legacy of Pandita Ramabai*. With Sebastian Kim & Rajkumar Boaz Johnson, Delhi, MIIS & ISPCK, 2011.
- *Missiology for the 21st Century: South Asian Perspectives*. With Paul Joshua Bhakiaraj. Delhi, MIIS & ISPCK, 2004.

- *Christianity Is Indian: The Emergence of an Indigenous Community*. Delhi, MIIS & ISPCK, 2000; Revised 2004.
- *Carey's Obligation & India's Renaissance*. With J. T. K. Daniel, Serampore, Council of Serampore College, 1993.
- *Many Other Names? Questions of Religious Pluralism*. A Symposium by R. Hedlund, P. B. Thomas, Martin Alphonse, George David. Delhi, ISPCK,
- *Culture and Evangelization*. With Beulah Herbert. Madras, CGRC, 1984.
- *India Church Growth*. With Kumar Doss & Beulah Herbert. Madras, CGRC, 1984.
- *Indigenous Missions of India*. With F. Hrangkhuma. Madras, Church Growth Research Centre, 1980.
- *World Christianity- South Asia*. Monrovia, MARC/World Vision, 1980.
- *Church Growth in the Third World*. Bombay, GLS, 1977.

*Essays Published in Collections:*

- "Fourth Branch Christianity: Indigeneity, Contextuality, Pentecostalism, and Independent Christian Movements" in *A Cultured Faith: Essays in Honour of Prof. G.P.V. Somaratna on his Seventieth Birthday* edited by Prabo Mihindukulasuriya, Ivor Poobalan and Ravin Caldera. Colombo Theological Seminary, 2011.
- "Present-day Independent Christian Movements: A South Asian Perspective" in *Christian Movements in Southeast Asia: A Theological Exploration* edited by Michael Nai-Chiu Poon, Singapore, Trinity Theological College, 2010.
- "Understanding Southeast Asian Christianity" in *Christian Movements in Southeast Asia: A Theological Exploration* edited by Michael Nai-Chiu Poon, Singapore, Trinity Theological College, 2010.
- "Hindu-Christian Relationships" in *Global Dictionary of Theology* edited by William A. Dyrness and Veli-Matti Kärkäinnen, Illinois, IVP Academic, 2008.

- "New Testament Perspectives on Mission" and "Homogeneous Unit" in *Dictionary of Mission Theology: Evangelical Foundations* edited by John Corrie, Illinios, Inter-Varsity Press, 2007.
- "Evangelical Christians and Social Transformation" in *Integral Mission the Way Forward: Essays in Honour of Dr. Saphir P. Athyal* edited by C.V. Mathew, Kerala, Christava Sahitya Samithi, 2006.
- "Indigenous Pentecostalism in India" in *Asian and Pentecostal: The Charismatic Face of Christianity in Asia* edited by Allan Anderson and Edmond Tang, Regnum Books International and APTS Press, Oxford/Baguio, 2005.
- "The Importance of the Study of India's New Christian Movements" in *New Wineskins: The New Indigenous Missions of Coastal Andhra Pradesh* by P. Solomon Raj, 2003.
- "Emerging Indigenous Christianity in India and Asia (19th and 20th Centuries)" in *Transkontinentale Beziehungen in Der Geschichte Des Aussereuropäischen Christentums* edited by Klaus Koschorke, 2002.
- "20th Century Mission Conferences: Models for Engagement with Hinduism and Islam" in *The Indian Church in Context* edited by Mark T. B. Laing, 2002.
- "Response to Persecution and Suffering in the History of Christian Mission" in *Persecution and Suffering: Christian Reflections and Responses* edited by Mark T. B. Laing, 2002.
- "Indian Instituted Churches: Indigenous Christianity Indian Style" in *Churches of Indigenous Origins in Northeast India* edited by O. L. Snaitang, 2000.
- "The Search for Indigenous Church Models in India" in *Mission & Missions: Essays in Honour of I. Ben Wati* edited by Jey J. Kanagaraj, UBS, 1998.
- "The Need for Cross-Cultural Mission in India Today" in *Church Ministry and Mission, Essays in Honour of K. Imotemjen Aier* edited by Renthy Keitzar, 1988.

- "Contextualized Protestant Missionary Training" in *Missions & Theological Education in World Perspective* edited by Harvie M. Conn and Samuel F. Rowen, 1984.
- "Christian Freedom and Third World Realities" in *Christian Freedom: Essays in Honor of Vernon C. Grounds* edited by K.W. M. Wozniak & Stanley Grenz, 1986.
- "A New Partnership for Mission" in *Readings in Third World Missions* edited by Marlin L. Nelson, 1976.

*Recent Articles Published:*

- "Methodology in Missiology." *Journal of the Colombo Theological Seminary*, Kohuwela, Sri Lanka, Vol. VI, 2010, 39-46.
- "Edinburgh Continuation Conferences in Asia." *Dharma Deepika* Issue 31, Vol.14, No.1, January-June 2010.
- "The Importance of the Study of India's New Christian Movements." *Journal of the Colombo Theological Seminary* Vol. V, 2009, 5-24.
- "Hindus and Christians Together for 2000 Years." Published under "Featured Articles" at www.globalmissiology.org, January 2008.
- "Indigenous Peoples of South Asia." *Dharma Deepika* Issue 27, Vol. 12, No.1, January-June 2008.
- "Critique of Pentecostal Mission by a Friendly Evangelical." *Asian Journal of Pentecostal Studies* Vol. 8, 1 January 2005.
- "The Witness of New Christian Movements in India." Posted Paper, International Association of Mission Studies (IAMS Assembly) Conference, Malaysia 31 July-7 August 2004.
- "Indian Expressions of Indigenous Christianity." *Studies in World Christianity* (The Edinburgh Review) 10, 2, 2004.
- "Previews of Christian Indigeneity in India." *Journal of Asian Mission,* 3(2), 2001.

- "Approaches to Indian Church History in Light of New Christian Movements." *Indian Church History Review*, December 2000.
- "The Need for a Major Ecumenical Reference Work on Christianity in South Asia." *Missiology, An International Review* Vol. XXVII, 1 January 1999.
- "Indian Christians of Indigenous Origins and Their Solidarity with Original Groups." *Journal of Dharma* Vol. XXIV, 1 1999.
- "Subaltern Movements and Indian Churches of Indigenous Origins." *Journal of Dharma* Vol. XXII, 1, 1998.
- "Missiological Issues in the Study of Christianity." *Ishvani Documentation and Mission Digest* Vol. XV, No.2, May-Aug, 1997: 94-107.
- "Christian Missionary Records in Calcutta." *Dharma Deepika* Vol.1, No.2, 1995.
- "Journals as Sources for Missiological Research." *Dharma Deepika* Vol.1, 1, 1995.
- "Something on Evangelism in Mega-Cities of the Indian Sub-Continent." *Journal of the Academy for Evangelism in Theological Education*. Vol. 9, 1993-1994.
- "William Carey, A Missiologist Before Time." *Indian Church History Review*. 1993.
- "William Carey, Some Unusual Facts." *Christian History*. 1992.
- "Geography of the Christian World Mission." *Ishvani Documentation Digest*. 1991.

## Indian Christianity: An Alternate Reading

The present volume is an introduction to Christianity in India. As mentioned in the introduction by the author, the approach in this book is non-technical and I am sure this book will be accepted well not only by the academic community but also by the general readers.

The book is a descriptive study of some aspects of Christianity in India during its long history from the first to the twenty-first century. The author selectively refers to and writes about significant events, personalities and developments of the Church in India. India is a large country comprising of different regions with a history of the church that is as old as Christianity itself, especially in South India. There are other churches which are younger and yet vibrant and energetic. A case in point is the churches in the Northeast India. The churches are growing also in the west, the north and the central India at a rapid pace. These are great days in Indian Church history. In such a context of growth and expansion, it is not easy to be selective when one is dealing with a subject matter like history of the Church. The author has done justice by selecting and describing the most significant events, the key figures and developments in the history of the church in India in this book.

An important contribution of this book is that instead of beginning with the so-called 'great traditions'- those of the elite hierarchical, and the professional officialdom of the church, the author looks at the 'little tradition'. This is what he means by the alternate reading. In this book, one will find references to sources that reflect expressions 'from below'. This historiography from below pays attention to the empirical data drawn from participants in the drama. It acknowledges the complexity of Indian Christianity and honours the multiple cultural identities of the church in India. The book is clearly written in a readable style and is a valuable resource for teachers and students of church history, and for all those who are interested in learning about the Indian Church.

I congratulate Dr. Hedlund for presenting this thought provoking book to the Church in India.

**Rev. Dr. Takatemjen**
Principal, Clark Theological College

# Foreword-2

The origin of Christianity in India has been the subject of controversy among historians owing to the near absence of documentary evidences for the first few centuries. The Christian message is claimed to have been brought to India by St. Thomas and St. Bartholomew, two apostles of Jesus Christ. It is to be noted that this has been the constant tradition of the Syrian Christians of Malabar, and it has been widely believed in the west also that St. Thomas' field of work was India. The congregations of South Indian Christians in particular have always prided themselves in the long-standing tradition that their Christianity is apostolic and that it was introduced in Malabar by the Apostle Thomas. There are number of evidences and traditions that support the apostolic Christianity in India that makes the study of the history of Christianity in India thrilling and profoundly interesting.

The history of Christianity in India has until recently been treated as an eastward extension of western ecclesiastical history. However, there are now efforts to write the history of Christianity in the socio-political and cultural context of the Indian people. The remarkable contributions made by the western missionaries in the expansion of Christianity in India cannot be simply ignored. However, the contributions made by the native Indians for the growth of Christianity in the soil of India is to be treated important for the understanding of the history of Christianity in India. Church history in India will have a greater value through the understanding of the roles played by the several key figures as intensively discussed in this book.

Indian Christianity: An Alternative Reading, authored by Roger E. Hedlund, is a well-documented book supported by rich and authentic sources covering the first to the twenty-first century. It clearly projects the rich heritage of Indian Christianity. I appreciate and congratulate the author for bringing out this book, which would offer new insights to the readers and be a great informative read. This book will definitely be a help for anyone in the better understanding of the history of Christianity in India.

**Rev. Dr. Marnungsang**
Associate Prof. of History of Christianity &
Dean of Post-Graduate Studies
Clark Theological College

# Acknowledgements

Writing is not done in a vacuum. In this introductory study, I have utilized the work of numerous scholars and well-informed sources whose contributions, references and ideas are carefully documented in the footnotes of each chapter. Chapter one is based on an earlier essay written for the Correspondence Section of the Department of Christian Studies in the University of Madras. Portions of chapter fourteen appeared in a paper, 'Challenges to Mission in the 21st Century', presented as part of the Tambaram IMC Platinum Jubilee (1938-2013) at Madras Christian College, Chennai, 13-14 December 2013.These and other similar instances of possible overlap have been noted and documented in the footnotes.

With appreciation I acknowledge the encouragement and helpful suggestions received from Robert Eric Frykenberg, Professor Emeritus of History & South Asian Studies at the University of Wisconsin, Madison; and by Professor Thom Wolf of the University Institute, New Delhi; also a special thanks for the valuable assistance of the love of my life and best friend, Thea June Hedlund, without whose help this project would have been further delayed and might never have come to publication.

I acknowledge my debt to Mr. Mitadru Basu, New Delhi, who first proposed the idea and requested me to write a non-technical introduction to Christianity in India.

Special thanks to friends in Nagaland, particularly Rev. Dr. Takatemjen Ao, my old student, now Principal of Clark Theological

College, Aolijen, Mokokchung, for undertaking the publication of this volume. May you together with other friends throughout North East India and beyond be blessed through the reading of this small volume.

To these and other unnamed friends who in various ways contributed to this volume, many thanks and appreciation.

**Roger E. Hedlund**
13 October, 2015

# Historiography

This book is a descriptive study of some of the aspects of Christianity in India during its long history from the first to the twenty-first century. Significant events, personalities and developments are here. But there is much more than can be told in this brief introduction to the subject. For further reading the concluding chapter offers a number of important sources such as volumes on the history of Christianity in India as well as the bibliography which follows.

This study follows an approach somewhat similar to that of Wendy Doniger's 'Foreword' in *Popular Christianity in India: Riting Between the Lines* edited by Selva J. Raj and Corinne G. Dempsey (Albany: State University of New York Press, 2002). Sources utilized tend to be those reflecting popular expressions of Christianity 'from below', the 'little tradition', rather than those of the elite hierarchical, professional officialdom of the 'great tradition'. This historiography from below—empirical data drawn from participants—acknowledges the complexity of Indian Christianity and honours the multiple cultural identities of Indian Christians.

# Introduction

**Indian Christianity: An Alternate Reading** is an introductory study of some of the highlights of Indian Christianity beginning with its central figure, Jesus of Nazareth, followed by the Apostle Thomas who is believed to have brought to India the Good News about Jesus in the first century AD.

The Indianness of Christianity in India is its distinguishing mark. This being true, an extensive diversity notwithstanding, each facet bears an Indian imprint. India in the 21st century thus makes a significant contribution to World Christianity. *World* Christianity stands in contrast to *global* Christianity. Globalisation is indeed an important aspect in Christianity's spread. But it is not the Eurocentric Western model that is spreading. In the era of the third millennium, Christianity is arising in a multitude of colours and forms from Asia as well as from Africa, Latin America and the Pacific region. Indigenous expressions of faith are clearly rooted in their respective cultures, yet explicitly 'Christian' in their confession of the Lordship of Jesus Christ. Indian Christianity is of apostolic origin, and its multiplied manifestations are in historical continuity with the stream of faith flowing from New Testament times into our own.

Through the centuries Indian Christianity has experienced renewal through encounter with a succession of other Christian traditions making their way to India. Each of these has made an impact in India, more importantly Christianity has been enriched by India. The incarnational Christianity of India, characterised by its Indianness, makes a distinctly Indian contribution to World Christianity. Several key figures are introduced as well as significant movements, developments and events through which Indian Christianity affirms the apostolicity, diversity, catholicity, historicity and missional nature of the church of Jesus Christ.

# Contents

Chapter 1

# At the Beginning
# Who is Jesus Christ?[1]

To understand Christianity we need first to consider its founder. Who was this first century figure, Jesus of Nazareth?

## Introduction

Jesus of Nazareth was a controversial figure! Who is Jesus? Jesus was not a theologian. He was not an ascetic monk. Neither was he a priest, nor a bishop or administrator. 'Jesus was a layman, an itinerant preacher and a popular story teller who depended on friends for meals and lodging.'[2] Not a revolutionary as we think of one today, he nevertheless inspired a revolutionary movement which continues to grow and spread.

The dispute is not about his life and teachings, the controversy concerns who Jesus is. The earliest Christians believed that there

1 A longer version of this chapter appeared as Unit 1: Who is Jesus for Christians? Paper VI: The Person and Message of Jesus. M. A. Christian Studies by Correspondence, Department of Christian Studies, University of Madras, 2003.

2 Carl E. Braaten, *The Flaming Center*, Philadelphia, Fortress Press, 1977, 74.

is only one God, and they worshipped Jesus Christ as God. The controversy rages over the claim 'that in the human person of Jesus, God Himself has come among us in a decisive and unrepeatable way.'[3] This claim is at the heart of Christian belief.

In the New Testament the Fourth Gospel (John) begins by presenting Jesus as the eternal God. John takes us back into eternity before the beginning of history to reveal the glory of God in Christ. 'In the beginning was the Word, and the Word was with God, and the Word was God. He was in the beginning with God; all things were made through Him, and without Him was not anything made that was made'(John 1:1-3). In John's language, the Word is the expression of God in personal form.[4] 'And the Word became flesh and dwelt among us, full of grace and truth; we have beheld his glory, glory as of the only Son from the Father' (John 1:14). The climax of the introduction to John's Gospel is in this statement of the incarnation.

## The Incarnation

The incarnation is a theological statement about who Jesus is. The incarnation concerns the enfleshment of God. Fully God and fully human: how could it be? Theologians have struggled to express the significance of this mystery. In essence the incarnation says that God in Christ continues forever to be both God and human, two natures but one person. 'Our Lord Jesus Christ has, from eternity, and has never ceased to have, all the attributes of Deity. Since His incarnation He has, and will never cease to have, all the essential attributes of humanity.'[5]

Jesus Himself expressed His oneness with God in a series of 'I am' sayings in the Fourth Gospel. 'I am the bread of life' (John 6:35); 'I am the light of the world' (8:12); 'Before Abraham was, I am'

3 Howard Peskett & Vinoth Ramachandra, *The Message of Mission: The Glory of Christ in All Time and Space*, Delhi, ISPCK and Chennai, MIIS, 2003, 18.

4 Francis Breisch, *The Ministry of Christ*, Grand Rapids, 1963, 43.

5 J. Oliver Buswell, *A Systematic Theology of the Christian Religion*, Vol. II, Part III, Grand Rapids, Zondervan, 1962, 69.

(8:58); 'I am the door of the sheep' (10:7); 'I am the good shepherd' (10:11); 'I am the Son of God' (10:36); 'I am the resurrection and the life' (11:25); 'I am the way, the truth, and the life' (14:6). Jesus borrows language and statements of the Old Testament, especially from the Prophecy of Isaiah, which speak of Yahweh (God) as the only God and Savior, and applies them to Himself. By doing this Jesus claims for Himself the very nature of God.[6]

The incarnation tells us that Jesus always existed because He is God, and that at a certain point in time God in Jesus entered human history. The meaning of this event is explained further in other writings of the New Testament. In the Epistle to the Colossians, St. Paul elucidates, 'He is the image of the invisible God, the first-born of all creation; for in Him all things were created.... He is before all things, and in Him all things hold together' (Col.1:15-17). Jesus as Creator is a further expression of his deity. 'For in Him all the fullness of God was pleased to dwell' (Col.1:19). This is the heart of the Christian concept of incarnation.

The Jesus of the New Testament was a real man. There was never any question about his humanity. The people of Judea and Galilee in first century Palestine who were his neighbors and followers knew about His birth and parentage. Jesus of Nazareth was a first century Jew born in Bethlehem, who lived a human life of joy and sorrow, and who died a violent human death.

How, then, is Jesus different from other humans, from other religious leaders? Consider His message: He proclaimed the Kingdom of God as an event now being fulfilled. Consider His deeds: His miracles were demonstrations of the powerful presence of the Kingdom of God. Consider His teachings: His parables and words were an invitation to exclusive discipleship. Above all is the reality of the resurrection. Three days after his crucifixion, death and burial, Jesus was alive again. 'Christianity could not have come into

6 David M. Ball, "'My Lord and My God': The Implications of the 'I Am' Sayings for Religious Pluralism" in *One God, One Lord in a World of Religious Pluralism* edited by Andrew D. Clarke and Bruce W. Winter, Cambridge, Tyndale House, 1991, 64.

being unless Jesus had really existed. Equally certainly, it would never have come into being unless people had believed in His resurrection. And this belief could not have arisen if the resurrection was not itself a historical event'.[7] The resurrection of Jesus is the touchstone of Christian faith.

For Christians, the understanding of Jesus as Redeemer and Lord underlines the purpose of Jesus' coming. Jesus is the Saviour, born to 'save His people from their sins' (Matthew 1:21).

## The Saviour

Jesus claimed to be the Saviour of the world. 'I came', said he, 'not to judge the world, but to save it' (John 12:47). Following Jesus' discourse with Nicodemus about the necessity of spiritual rebirth, John declared that 'God sent the Son into the world, not to condemn the world, but that the world might be saved through Him' (3:17). In His conversation with Zacchaeus, whose conversion and transformation is recorded in Luke's Gospel, Jesus stated, 'For the Son of man came to seek and to save the lost' (Luke 19:10).

Jesus in John's Gospel announced that when He is 'lifted up' He will draw all humans to Himself (John 12:32) by which He alluded to His approaching death on the cross (John 8:28; 3:14). Salvation in the New Testament is linked with the Cross. The Cross as much as the incarnation makes Jesus' mission unique. According to St. Paul, Christ brought reconciliation 'by making peace through the blood of his cross' (Colossians 1:20). An amazing proposition! In the Roman Empire crucifixion, though widespread, was viewed with universal horror and disgust. It was cruel and degrading, the most humiliating form of death in the ancient world. 'For the Jews a crucified Messiah/Saviour was a contradiction in terms, for it expressed not God's power but God's inability to liberate Israel from Roman rule. For pagans, the idea that a god or son of god should die as a state criminal, and

7 Howard Marshall, 'Who was Jesus?' in *Eerdmans' Handbook to Christian Belief*, Grand Rapids, 1982, 57.

that human salvation should depend on that particular historical event, was not only offensive; it was sheer *madness*'.[8]

Nevertheless, it was this message which the disciples of Jesus proclaimed, and which has continued to spread bringing life and hope to multitudes. The preaching of the New Testament apostles centered in the cross and resurrection.

The entire New Testament bears witness to Jesus Christ as Saviour of the world. His disciples carried the message to South and North, West and East, thus even to India in the first century according to the accepted St.Thomas traditions. The message of the cross and resurrection have continued to be spread by the followers of Christ in the succeeding generations.

## Prophet, Priest and King

Jesus in biblical and theological consideration is to be seen not in isolation but as the culmination of a succession of prophets. 'God in times past spoke to our fathers by the prophets' (Hebrews 1:1). The writer goes on to declare that now in the present God has spoken to us through Christ (Hebrews 1:2-14). Jesus does not call Himself a prophet, yet He was seen as a prophet by other people. Like the Old Testament prophets, Jesus performed miracles and symbolic actions, uttered promises and threats, was able to discern human thoughts, and foretold future events. Some New Testament passages depict Jesus as the promised prophet of the last days who brings salvation.[9]

The Qur'an, which includes Jesus among the prophets, also mentions Him as Messiah, son of Mary. Parrinder comments that Jesus' use of the designation 'Son of Man' points to his Messiahship. More problematic is the term 'Son of God' which must be shorn of any physical paternity connotations. When Jesus addresses God as 'Father' it is an expression of the closest possible relationship

8 Peskett & Ramachandra, *The Message of Mission*, 25-26.

9 G. Friedrich, "Prophet" in *Theological Dictionary of the New Testament* edited by Gerhard Kittel and Gerhard Friedrich, Abridged in One Volume by Geoffrey W. Bromiley, Grand Rapids, Eerdmans, 1985, 962.

between God and humankind, with no sensual implications.[10] The title 'prophet' should be seen in connection with other titles such as Son of Man, Lord, and Son of God, which together designate Jesus as Messiah. Jesus is Messiah, Christ, the Anointed One. Peter's sermons in the Book of Acts point to Jesus as Messiah and Saviour. The Messiah saves those who repent and believe. 'The proclamation of the Messiah was the proclamation of salvation.'[11]
Christ as Priest is elaborately presented in the Epistle to the Hebrews. Here, Christ is enthroned as the great high priest who offered Himself once for all as a sacrifice to take away sins forever (Hebrews 4:14; 6:20; 7:27; 9:12,26; 10:10-12).

Theologians tend to combine the three offices of Prophet, Priest and King into one doctrine of Christ as Mediator. Jesus Christ as Mediator intervenes between God and humans to establish peace. 'There is one God, and there is one mediator between God and humankind, the man Christ Jesus, who gave Himself as a ransom for all' (1 Timothy 2:5-6). On the basis of His sacrifice of Himself, Jesus brings God and humans together. 'The mystery of Jesus Christ unveils to us the mystery of God.... In Jesus Christ, the Word of God has entered human history personally'.[12]

There also are other models, which help us to understand the mystery of Jesus.

## Jesus of History, Christ of Faith

Theologians of the past struggled over the vexed question of how to explain the two natures in one person of the God-man Jesus Christ. 'The first fact of Christianity is Jesus of Nazareth; add to Him the title Christ and we have the formula that has been the bone of contention among theologians'.[13] But, neither the Gospel records

---

10 Geoffrey Parrinder, *Jesus in the Qur'an,* New York, Oxford University Press, 1977, 129-130.

11 William M. Ramsay, *The Christ of the Earliest Christians*, Richmond, John Knox Press, 1959, 41.

12 Jacques Dupuis, *Who Do You Say I Am?* Maryknoll, Orbis, 1994, 169.

13 Fernandez, *In Ways Known to God*, 212.

nor the theologizing found in the New Testament epistles, ever distinguish between Jesus and His messianic title. The identity of Jesus as the Christ is clearly spelled out in the famous *kenosis* passage in Paul's Epistle to the Philippians:

> Christ Jesus, who, though He was in the form of God, did not count equality with God a thing to be grasped, but emptied Himself, taking the form of a servant, being born in the likeness of men. And being found in human form He humbled Himself and became obedient unto death, even death on a cross (Philippians 2:5-8).

Jesus of Nazareth is the Christ of faith according to Scripture. 'St. Paul did not set aside the historical Jesus in favor of a spiritual or mystical Christ: He knew only one Jesus, who was crucified, rose again and now lives forever'.[14] Salvation in the New Testament is proffered in and through the historic person of Jesus Christ, the incarnate Son of God, not a mythological demi-god.

True, Gandhiji and the great Radhakrishnan were among some who did not consider the historicity of Jesus to be important but still appreciated His examples and teachings. The Indian theologian Chenchiah tried to extract Jesus from the accretion of Church dogmas, and others want to opt for His spirituality without historicity. But, as Robin Boyd states, we need both history and experience. 'It is the *same* Jesus who once walked in Galilee who today claims my life, and gives me the power of His Spirit'.[15]

The only Jesus we know anything about is the Jesus of the four Gospels. It is this historic Jesus who is identified by the Gospel writers and by the earliest Christians as Christ, the promised Messiah of Israel and Saviour of the world. The Christ of faith *is* the Jesus of history.

---

14 Leon-Dufour cited by Fernandez, op.cit., 212.

15 Boyd, *Khristadvaita*, 117.

## Conclusion

Who is Jesus Christ? The witness of Scripture is that He is Lord. This is the conclusion of St. Paul who anticipates the ultimate Lordship of Christ over everything: 'God has highly exalted Him and bestowed on Him the name which is above every name, that at the name of Jesus every knee should bow, in heaven and on earth and under the earth, and every tongue confess that Jesus Christ is Lord, to the glory of God the Father' (Philippians 2:9-11). The title 'Lord' expresses Christ's rule over all. This title was used 222 times by St. Paul. In the Old Testament 'Lord' was used in place of the sacred name of God, Yahweh. 'Lord' is a common designation used in the worship of God.[16] The Christian understanding of Jesus is compressed in the title 'Lord'. The confession of St. Thomas, erstwhile doubter and eventual Apostle to India, sums it all up: 'My Lord and my God!' (John 20:28)

16 Chris Byworth, "The Names and Titles of Jesus" in *Eerdmans' Handbook to Christian Belief*, Grand Rapids, 1982, 82.

Chapter 2

# Foundations
# Thomas and the First Christians

The story of Indian Christianity begins in the first century AD with the arrival of the Apostle Thomas. In the town of Parur, in the South Indian State of Kerala, the old church of Kottakkavu is said to be the site at which Thomas founded the first Christian church in India in AD 52.[1] According to tradition Thomas arrived in AD 52, preached the gospel and established churches in Kerala, then traveled to the East coast where he was martyred (at a place now known as St. Thomas Mount). His body was brought to Mylapore and laid to rest in a tomb, which is maintained and accessible at the San Thome Cathedral.

## Thomas Tradition

The story of Thomas Christianity is of great significance for the history of Christianity in India. As historian Stephen Neill states, despite a lack of absolute certainty, there is a high degree of probability

1 Andrew Todhunter, 'In the Footsteps of the Apostles', *National Geographic,* March 2012, 47.

that by the sixth century there were well-established churches in South India and that this community had been strengthened by a Christian immigration in the fourth century. It is also probable that at least a section of the indigenous Indian church originated in the Tamil region. The Christian community in Kerala appears to have been prosperous and enjoying the favour of local rulers.[2] These and other factors suggest the strongest possibility that the Apostle Thomas could have come to India and that the church in Kerala dates back to him. 'Kerala's Thomas Christians — like Christians elsewhere in Asia and in Africa and Latin America — have made the faith uniquely their own, incorporating traditional art, architecture, and natural symbolism'.[3] The very 'Indianness' of Thomas Christianity in itself supports the hypothesis of their apostolic origin.

The ancient Christian community of India together with similar communities in other parts of Asia comprise the extensive 'Eastern Christianity' of Syria, Armenia, Iraq, Iran and India in contrast to the 'Western Christianity' of the Greek and Latin world of Europe. Many of the Christian communities of Asia disappeared with the rise of Islam, although some continued to exist in weakened form, but not so in India 'where Christian life has remained vigorous' for the past twenty centuries.[4]

## Apostolic Christianity

Kerala is recognised as the birthplace of Christianity in India. Christianity is one of the ancient religions of India, as India's first Prime Minister, Pundit Jawaharlal Nehru, pointed out. The story has been told and retold in multiplied publications. The Church History Association of India (CHAI) devotes more than 100 pages in the first volume of its History of Christianity in India series to the Thomas tradition and questions concerning the origins and history of the

---

2 Stephen Neill, *A History of Christianity in India: The Beginnings to AD 1707*, Cambridge University Press, Cambridge, 1984, 48-49.

3 Todhunter, 'In the Footsteps of the Apostles', 47.

4 Leonard Fernando and G. Gispert-Sauch, eds., *Christianity in India: Two Thousand Years of Faith*, New Delhi: Viking Penguin, 2004, 57.

earliest Christians in India. According to the best-received traditions, Christianity has existed here from Apostolic (first century) times. Historically, Christianity has a respected presence in India from the earliest times. The vibrant Thomas Christian community itself is custodian of countless oral traditions preserving the Thomas saga in story and song. Kerala's Christianity is not only an ancient religion of India, it is one of the earliest Churches in the world. The presence of apostolic Christianity in India from the very beginning refutes the notion that Christianity is a foreign religion imported by missionaries and colonialists. History tells otherwise. Christianity was firmly planted in Indian soil long before it arrived in Northern Europe. Belief in their Apostolic origin is a deep-rooted tradition among the Thomas Christians and helped them to preserve their Christian identity and faith.[5]

The existence of oral traditions as well as palm-leaf manuscripts, copper-plates, stone inscriptions and other artifacts preserved by leading families attest the antiquity and authenticity of the Thomas Christian community. 'Many Thomas Christian families of Kerala still trace the original conversion of their community to the time of the Apostle, or to any of a number of migrations which occurred during the many centuries prior to the arrival of the Portuguese in 1498'.[6]

Who were these original Indian Christians? Tradition has it that among Thomas' converts were several Brahmans. If so, this helps to explain the caste-like status accorded the early Christian community whose customs and practices were similar to those of the surrounding Hindus. Also not to be overlooked is a significant Jewish element. A diaspora Jewish colony, dating from the Old Testament period, was located in Cranganore and was engaged in trade with the Mediterranean world. Exact date of the first Jewish settlement is

5 Francis Thonippara, 'St. Thomas Christians: The First Indigenous Church of India' in *Christianity is Indian: The Emergence of an Indigenous Community* edited by Roger E. Hedlund, Delhi: ISPCK, Chennai: MIIS, revised 2004, 61.

6 Robert Eric Frykenberg, *Christianity in India: From Beginnings to the Present*, New York: Oxford University Press, 2008, 101.

not definite, and there are several conflicting theories. In any event, the Jews found in Cranganore a haven of refuge and a centre for trade, and evidence indicates such a settlement existed during the first century of the Christian era.[7] According to one tradition, the Apostle Thomas arrived in a trading vessel from Alexandria. If so, it is entirely possible that the Apostle found ready converts among the Jewish settlers. These early Jewish Christian converts, believed in Jesus as the Christ, but also retained Jewish traditions and called themselves *Nazrani* as Jewish disciples of Jesus of Nazareth whom they accepted as the promised Messiah.[8]

Conflicting theories not withstanding, the Thomas Christians maintained a distinct identity with lifestyle, customs, traditions and a respectable social status borrowed from the Hindu environment. The Thomas Christians were no threat to their Hindu neighbours. The Christians were a small minority who learned to live at peace with the larger community. The *Nazrani* apparently did not seek conversions from other castes, and this enabled them to survive.[9] Rightly or wrongly, Hinduism often is perceived as accommodating and tolerant. Certainly throughout India's long history at various times different religious groups learned to live side by side. Not so much tolerance, perhaps, as 'an inclusivistic tendency that accommodates other religious groups by absorbing their basic beliefs as one's own'.[10] This being so, the survival and Christian identity of the ancient Thomas community is amazing. Among the many explanatory factors one must consider the 'Syrianisation' of the Thomas Christians.

---

7 S. S. Koder, 'Kerala and Her Jews', (a short history), Cochin Synagogue, Mattancheri, Kerala, n.d., 1, 3.

8 New World Encyclopedia contributors, 'Saint Thomas Christians', *New World Encyclopedia,* http://www.newworldencyclopedia.org/entry/Saint_Thomas_Christians?oldid=747830 (accessed October 17, 2011).

9 Anand Amaladass, 'Dialogue between Hindus and the St. Thomas Christians' in *Hindu-Christian Dialogue: Perspectives and Encounters,* edited by Harold Coward, Motilal Banarsidass Publishers, Delhi, 1993, 16-17.

10 Ibid., 18.

## Syrian Connection

Migrating 'Syrian' Christians from Persia arriving in Malabar, India, in the fourth century (345 AD), came into direct contact with the Indian Christian community with whom they interacted and amalgamated thus reinvigorating the Indian Christian community. Indian Christianity, however, pre-dated the arrival of Christians from Persia. The Indian church already existed and had a long and independent history of its own. 'Indian Christianity is as old as Christianity itself'.[11]

The Christian migrants from Persia were not so much Persian as 'Syrian' having connections going back to Antioch and the use of 'Syriac' as their language of worship. The origin of Christianity in Persia, shrouded in legend, includes a Thomas tradition. One immigrant group associated with Thomas of Cana, a Syrian merchant, in the fourth century brought spiritual resurgence – and prosperity — to the declining Thomas Christian community in India. Welcomed by the Thomas Christians, the Syrians nevertheless retained a distinct identity. Subsequently emerged two streams of Malabar Christians: The 'Northists' descending from Christians of St. Thomas, the 'Southists' from Thomas of Cana.[12]

The connection between the Church in India and Syrian-Persian Christianity began in the third or fourth century. Gradually everything ecclesiastical in India became essentially East-Syrian. This preserved a strong Christian tradition, but at the cost of preventing the Indian church from developing a distinctly *Indian* Christian culture.[13] By the fifth century 'the ecclesiastical ties between Persia and the Christians of India were regularised and strengthened' resulting in use of Syriac

---

11 Thonippara, 'St. Thomas Christians: The First Indigenous Church of India' in *Christianity is Indian: The Emergence of an Indigenous Community*, 62.

12 A. M. Mundadan, *From the Beginning Up to the Middle of the Sixteenth Century*, Bangalore: Church History Association of India, 1989, 64; also see Leslie Brown, *The Indian Christians of St. Thomas*, Cambridge & New York: Cambridge University Press, 1982.

13 Mundadan, *From the Beginning Up to the Middle of the Sixteenth Century*, 115.

as their ecclesiastical language as well as hierarchical dependency on the Persian Church.[14] The reinforcements brought fresh vigour, but gradually the original Indian Christianity was eclipsed, absorbed and Syrianised. This early modification has continued to the present time. Nevertheless, this ancient Syrian Christianity, which amalgamated with the earlier Indian Christian community is of great historic importance as the locus of pre-Portuguese Christianity in India.[15]

Indian Christianity comprises an ancient community as well as a present entity, which is making an important cultural contribution as a moral and spiritual force in contemporary society. Today, at least six Syrian Christian denominations accept the Thomas apostolic tradition as to the origins of Christianity in India. These include the Orthodox Syrian Church (in two sections), the Independent Syrian Church of Malabar (Kunnamkulam Diocese), the (Reformed) Mar Thoma Church, the Malankara (Syrian Rite) Catholic Church, the (Chaldean) Church of the East, and the St. Thomas Evangelical Church as well as a section of the Church of South India.[16] The institutions and personnel of India's ancient Christian community are an integral part of modern democratic India in which they continue to play a vital role. Syrian Christians were active in India's Independence movement, and continue to contribute to nation-building in diverse fields such as the arts, science and technology, linguistics, literature, education, social and political involvement.[17]

---

14 Samuel H. Moffett, *A History of Christianity in Asia*, Vol. I, Maryknoll: Orbis Books, 1998, 267-268.

15 Mar Aprem, *The Chaldean Syrian Church of the East*, Delhi: ISPCK, 1983.

16 See Leslie Brown, *The Indian Christians of St. Thomas*, Cambridge & New York: Cambridge University Press, 1982, for further information about the Thomas Christians including the story of its divisions.

17 Leonardo Fernando, 'Christian Contribution to Nation-Building' in the *Oxford Encyclopaedia of South Asian Christianity*, edited by R. E. Hedlund, J. M. Athyal, J. Kalapati and Jessica Richard, Oxford University Press, New Delhi, 2012.

## Plurality and Orality

From the beginning the Syrian Christians of Kerala shared a common world with the majority 'Hindu' population. The plural society of Kerala 'allowed for the interpenetration of Hindu, Christian and Syrian codes', states Visvanathan.[18] The Syrian Christians were seen as part of the Hindu caste system with accompanying notions of hierarchy, status and pollution. Their traditional occupation as traders, as well as landowners, gave the Syrian Christians a high caste status. Rituals and practices pertaining to occupation, food, marriage, birth and death likewise gave them a caste-like identity.[19]

The existence of oral traditions as well as palm-leaf manuscripts, copper-plates, stone inscriptions and other artifacts preserved by leading families attest the antiquity and authenticity of the Thomas Christian community. 'Many Thomas Christian families of Kerala still trace the original conversion of their community to the time of the Apostle, or to any of a number of migrations which occurred during the many centuries prior to the arrival of the Portuguese in 1498'.[20]

Oral traditions are of particular interest in light of the absence of documentary evidence from the earliest era. Historian D. Arthur Jeyakumar feels that the Western tradition (of Thomas travelling by overland trade routes and arriving in North India) is not sufficiently supported, but prefers the Indian Malabar tradition of Thomas in India which is an oral tradition passed down by word of mouth from generation to generation in story and song still today. The earliest documents that connect Thomas to India are from outside India, but from these sources we learn that it was commonly understood that Thomas had evangelised India where he also suffered martyrdom:

- *Doctrine of the Apostles* written in Edessa ca 250 AD, points to India as Thomas' the field of activity;

18 Susan Visvanathan, *The Christians of Kerala: History, Belief and Ritual among the Yakoba*, New Delhi: Oxford University Press, 1993, 1.

19 Ibid., 3.

20 Frykenberg, *Christianity in India*, 101.

- St. Ephraim, a hymn writer of Syria (d 373 AD), mentions the tradition of Thomas' mission in India in his hymn 'On Thomas the Apostle';
- St. Gregory of Mazianzen in the 4th century associates Thomas with India;
- St. Ambrose of Milan (333-397 AD), based on accounts of travellers as well as Greek and Latin classics, identified Thomas with India;
- Bishop Gregory of Tours (538-593 AD) in his book *In Gloria Martyrdom* mentions that Thomas was killed in India (and his remains brought to Edessa and buried there).[21]

**Documentation**

But there is more. The India/Malabar Tradition includes testimonials by outside visitors who encountered the Thomas Christians in Malabar or visited Thomas' tomb in Mylapore. These include Mar Solomon, a Nestorian Bishop who gives an account of the Thomas tradition in his *Book of the Bee* (1222); Marco Polo, the famous traveller from Venice, who gives an account of his visit to the site of Thomas' tomb (1292); John of Monte Corvino, a Franciscan monk who spent some time in India on his way to China, and mentions a 'Church of St. Thomas the Apostle' in a letter from Peking (8 January 1305); Odoric of Pordenone who, in an account of his travels in India (ca 1324), mentions the presence of Christians in a region where pepper grows and where the body of 'Blessed Thomas the Apostle' was laid to rest; John de Marignoli gave an account of his travels (1349 AD) through the province of India where the Church of St. Thomas was found and the Thomas Christians owned pepper gardens; one Nicolo de Conti who visited the Tomb of St. Thomas in a large and beautiful church of 'Nestorian heretics' numbering a thousand. Despite contradictions and inconclusive opinions, the tradition can be neither proven nor dis-proven, but it is entirely

21 D. Arthur Jeyakumar, *History of Christianity in India: Selected Themes*, Tamilnadu Theological Seminary, Arasaradi, Madurai, revised 2007, 7.

possible that St. Thomas could be the founder of Christianity in India.[22]

## Continuity

The essential point is that early in the era someone brought the gospel to India, and that Christianity has continuously existed in India since the earliest time. That Christianity is an ancient religion of India is proven historical fact. The reports given by visitors are of particular importance providing rare glimpses of the continuity of the Thomas Christians as a peaceful and prosperous community in South India during the thirteenth and fourteenth centuries.

22 D. Arthur Jeyakumar, *History of Christianity in India: Selected Themes*, Tamilnadu Theological Seminary, Arasaradi, Madurai, revised 2007, 9-10, 17.

Chapter 3

# Golden Era or Dark Age? The Silent Years Until the Portuguese Came

In *The Lost History of Christianity*, Philip Jenkins writes about what he calls *The Thousand-Year Golden Age of the Church in the Middle East, Africa, and Asia—and How It Died* [the sub-title of the book]. Increasingly Christian scholars are re-discovering a vibrant past history of the Church in Africa and Asia that is largely forgotten by the West. Certainly true with regard to India, some 40,000 thriving Christians in coastal India who had never heard of the Roman Pope; the Thomas Christians were an indigenous Malabar Church having its own hierarchy, a Syriac liturgy, and the Patriarch of Babylon as their spiritual head. With the coming of the Portuguese the Thomas Christians experienced controversy and eventual splits as Rome tried to absorb the ancient Apostolic community.[1]

1 Philip Jenkins, *The Lost History of Christianity: The Thousand-Year Golden Age of the Church in the Middle East, Africa, and Asia—and How It Died*, New York: Harper One, 2008, 67, 146-7.

## Lost History of Christianity in Asia?

Alternate Christianities existed. Nestorian missionaries traversed the legendary 'Silk Road' as did Monophysites and Manachaeans as well as Jacobites[2]. No one knows exactly when Christianity first reached China. But when Nestorian Christians came to China in 578 AD, they travelled along the Silk Road from Mesopotamia (present day Iran and Iraq).[3] Christian missionaries (monks) from Persia, utilising existing trade routes, reached China in 635 AD having travelled more than 4,000 miles through 'some of the most difficult terrain in the world'.[4] The so-called 'Silk Road' in actuality consisted not of one but of several parallel routes by which the Chinese (the first people to produce silk from silkworms) transported their highly priced commodity to the West. Part of the journey crossed an immense desert to the north of Tibet with intense sand storms and extreme variations in temperature impossible for humans to survive but for the two-humped Bactrian camel as a pack animal. 'This remarkable animal could cross the sand dunes of the Taklimakan, travel without water for two weeks at a time, and survive extremes of temperature while carrying loads of nearly 500 pounds'. Arrival of Christian missionaries in China in the seventh century 'was made possible by the existence of a vigorous missionary Church in Persia' who for purposes of evangelisation made use of the Silk Road to reach China and other 'trade routes on both shores of the Persian Gulf to Arabia and India'.[5]

Along the Silk Road, Nestorian 'merchants' would have encountered Mahayana Buddhist missionaries, and it is possible the two might have collaborated. Without forgetting their Semitic roots, Asian Churches adjusted to new cultures. Buddhist as well as Christian monasteries were established, symbols sometimes borrowed

---

2 Jenkins, *Lost History of Christianity*, 66-68.

3 Miriam Adeney, *Kingdom Without Borders: The Untold Story of Global Christianity*, Downers Grove: IV Press, 2009, 55.

4 Jean-Pierre Charbonnier, *Christians in China A.D. 600 to 2000*, San Francisco: Ignatius Press, 2007, 39.

5 Ibid., 41-43.

and adapted, such as a combined lotus-cross symbol used by the Nestorians to express the Christian message.[6] Eastern Christianity was bold and vibrant. Then something changed.

The change that brought about the collapse of Eastern Christianity in much of Asia was the coming of Islam. As Islam spread, Christians eventually were forced to submit. Ancient Asian Churches barely survived, mostly in name only in many Asian countries.[7] The Silk Road mission came to an end,[8] contributing to the isolation of Indian Christianity from the larger world beyond — this seclusion perhaps also a factor in the preservation of Indian Christianity.

Not everyone will agree with Jenkins' assessment of the era as the 'Golden Age' of Asian Christianity. Stephen Neill, for example, refers to this period as the 'Dark Age' of the Church. In a chapter by that title, Neill describes the eclipse of Eastern Christianity following Muslim conquests and control. As a result, in Neill's viewpoint, 'Christianity became an almost completely European religion'.[9] Even so, Christianity in Asia did not entirely disappear.

6 Jenkins, *Lost History of Christianity*, 92.

7 Ibid., 255.

8 The 'Silk Road' ended, but the idea was revived recently by the Chinese Church as a plan to send Chinese missionaries across Central Asia into the Middle East to re-evangelise the Muslim world and much more. A 'Back to Jerusalem' movement aims to send 100,000 Chinese missionaries beyond China to complete the task of world evangelisation! Chinese believers want to carry the gospel in the opposite direction along the Silk Road to plant churches in the Hindu world, the Buddhist world and the Muslim world, thence back to Jerusalem where it all began (Miriam Adeney, *Kingdom Without Borders: The Untold Story of Global Christianity*, Downers Grove: IVPress, 2009, 55). A Chinese spokesperson explained that Chinese missionaries will be part of the mainstream back to Jerusalem: 'We believe that now that the gospel has reached China it will follow the old Silk Road back to Jerusalem. Once the gospel comes back to Jerusalem, it will mean that the gospel has been preached to the whole world'(David Aikman, *Jesus in Beijing: How Christianity is Transforming China and Changing the Global Balance of Power*. Washington: Regnery, 2003, 203).

9 Stephen Neill, *A History of Christian Missions*, Baltimore: Penguin Books, 1964, 65.

As Neill also observes, the conquering Arabs needed the Christians (who were literate) to serve as clerks and translators in governmental administration.[10] Christians were granted second-class status, but required to pay a special tax, and other disabilities were imposed. Whether 'Golden' or 'Dark', it was also an age of discovery.

## The Vasco Da Gama Era

In 1498, Vasco da Gama arrived in Calicut, the beginning of the Portuguese presence in India. From then on there was considerable information recorded about Indian Christianity. Da Gama came to Malabar for pepper, and was primarily interested in trade. Nevertheless it was not long before the Portuguese made contact with the Thomas Christians. Cochin rather than Calicut was found more suitable—at the centre of the pepper fields and the Thomas Syrian Christians—and here da Gama established Portugal's first fort in India.[11] The Portuguese were explorers, adventurers, who also reported everything they saw—with or without proper understanding. Before long the Portuguese began to realise that the Thomas Christians were a different kind of Christian: Syriac rather than Latin liturgy, married rather than celibate priests, traced their apostolic heritage to Thomas rather than Peter, had no images in their churches, and did not recognise the pope as head of the Church. These 'deficiencies' the Portuguese Franciscan missionaries attempted to correct. However, as historian Moffett observes, 'Kerala's Christians never quite ceased to be other than Thomas Christians, however much some of them might adapt to the ways and traditions of the incoming Portuguese clergy'.[12]

## Francis Xavier

It was not in Kerala but in Goa where Portugal established its major base for trade. Goa also became the largest Roman Catholic Diocese

10 Neill, *History of Christian Missions,* 63.

11 Samuel H. Moffett, *A History of Christianity in Asia: Vol.II, 1500-1900,* Maryknoll: Orbis Books, 2005, 5.

12 Ibid., 6, 9.

beyond Europe. Initially the missionary priests were Franciscans, who also began the first seminary for training local religious. To Goa came also missionaries of the newly created Society of Jesus (Jesuits) founded in Paris in 1534 by Ignatius Loyola and confirmed by the Pope in 1540. In 1542, one of the original companions of Loyola, Francis Xavier (1506-1552), destined to become one of the greatest missionaries in Christian history, came to India under the authority of the Pope (as Papal Nuncio) and as the representative of the King of Portugal. Initially, Xavier set about reforming the depravity and nominal Christianity of Goa, but soon moved on to pursue his missionary calling among the Parava fisher community of the Coromandel Coast. Six years earlier, the entire Parava community had appealed to the Portuguese for protection, and had 'converted'—but were given no instruction and knew nothing as to the meaning of Christianity. The Paravas were scattered in villages over a two hundred mile coastal area, their catamarans their only means of livelihood. With the help of informants Xavier produced a crude translation of the Lord's Prayer, the Creed and the Ten Commandments into Tamil. Then, village by village, Xavier proceeded to teach these basics to the children. The children in turn by rote memory taught the elders, and the Sunday service consisted of line-by-line recitation of these elements. Inadequate and defective? Possibly. But apparently effective. Xavier's method laid a solid foundation, which endures into the present. 'By the end of the century, the Jesuits had gathered the Paravas into sixteen large villages, in each of which a Jesuit Father was resident. Discipline was stern...'.[13]

A number of families from other communities also were drawn into the Faith, as well as some 10,000 Mukkavars on the Western coast. 'These shoreline Christian communities retained their autonomy. Their religion, while Christian, remained conspicuously "Hindu" or "Nativistic". Ceremonials, rituals, and social structures remained "birth" and "caste" (*jati*) oriented'.[14] As Felix Wilfred observes, converts to Christianity, whether Catholic or Protestant,

13 Neill, *History of Christian Missions*, 150.

14 Frykenberg, *Christianity In India*, 138.

'actually practiced a latent religion in continuity with the Hindu tradition'.[15] This was so because the local people themselves 'tried to live Christianity in continuity with their religious tradition and social history'.[16] The 'Indianness' of Christianity is evident in the life and practices of these South Indian Christians.

## Roberto De Nobili

Catholic Christianity continued to expand beyond Goa. In 1605, a young Italian Jesuit, Roberto de Nobili, arrived in South India. After a few months on the Fishery Coast learning Tamil, Nobili was posted to the great centre of Tamil culture at Madurai. Here, Nobili immersed himself in the study of Tamil culture, philosophy and religion. In particular, he probed to discover reasons for the failure of the existing Madurai Mission, and discovered that the foreign lifestyle of the converts was repugnant to the cultured 'higher' castes of Madurai making it virtually impossible for the latter to even consider conversion. De Nobili decided on a radical experiment: 'To win the Indians he would become an Indian'.[17] He would eliminate wine, fish,meat and eggs from his diet, opting for a simple meal of rice, milk and vegetables prepared by a Brahman cook, wore wooden clogs in place of leather shoes, divested himself of the black cassock of the Catholic fathers for the saffron attire of a Hindu holy man.[18] For his accommodation of the local culture, Roberto de Nobili can be seen as an 'Indigenous Foreigner'.[19] Not only his personal lifestyle, Nobili's adaptations included liturgy and theology. Liturgical ceremonies were

15 Felix Wilfred, 'Christianity in Hindu Polytheistic Structural Mould: Converts in Southern Tamilnadu Respond to an Alien Religion during "the Vasco da Gama Epoch"', *Arch. De Sc. Soc. Des Rel., 1998,* 103 (juillet-septembre), 79.

16 Wilfred, 'Christianity in Hindu Polythesitic Structural Mould', 67.

17 Neill, *History of Christian Missions*, 184.

18 A. Sauliére, *His Star in the East*, revised by S. Rajamanickam, Anand: Gujarat Sahitya Prakash, 1995, 133-4.

19 See the essay by P. Peter Raj, 'Robert de Nobili: An Indigenous Foreigner' in *Christianity Is Indian: The Emergence of an Indigenous Community* edited by Roger E. Hedlund, Delhi: ISPCK, and Chennai: MIIS, revised 2004, 101-111.

inculturated, marriage and burial rites combined Christian traditions with Tamil customs. Christian theology should be expressed in local idiom for which Nobili devised new terms providing vocabulary for conveying Christian concepts.[20] Controversial for many—particularly by Portuguese ecclesiastical authorities who viewed his adaptations as a threat—Nobili experienced criticism, misunderstanding, betrayal and persecution.

De Nobili was a model of adaptation. His purpose was 'to show that the Christian faith could be thought and lived in a truly Indian way'.[21] His purpose was to demonstrate that 'it is possible to be Indian without being Hindu, and Christian without being European'.[22] A remarkable scholar and critical thinker, he wrote theological treatises in Tamil, and insisted that religion and culture can be separated. Nobili's approach was through the traditions of Hinduism. Those religious practices deemed incompatible with Christianity were removed, whereas the use of sandalwood paste, ritual baths and the threading ceremony were permitted. Other traditional practices were Christianised. It was de Nobili's conclusion that things exclusively devoted to idolatry cannot be permitted to Christians. Other customs could be continued, but questionable features should be discarded.[23]

The work of de Nobili four centuries ago seems relevant still today. In a study of de Nobili's *Responsio*, Anchukandam complains that 'The Catholic Church in India has not yet been able to present

---

20 See the essay by P. Peter Raj, 'Robert de Nobili: An Indigenous Foreigner' in *Christianity Is Indian: The Emergence of an Indigenous Community* edited by Roger E. Hedlund, Delhi: ISPCK, and Chennai: MIIS, revised 2004, 106.

21 F. X. Clooney, 'Roberto de Nobili's Response to India and Hinduism, In Practice and Theory', *Third Millennium* I (1998), 4, 73.

22 Ibid., 74.

23 S. Rajamanickam, *Roberto de Nobili on Indian Customs*, An Introduction by S. Rajamanickam and Translation of His *Informatio*, a Report about some Indian Social Customs, Palayamkottai: De Nobili Research Institute, St. Xavier's College, 1989. For further elaboration see Sauliére, *His Star in the East*, cited above.

itself to the Indians in an acceptable Indian form'.[24] The *Responsio* was Nobili's scholarly vindication of his adaptation policy that had occasioned bitter debate. The controversy was critical for the precarious future of a neophyte Church. De Nobili's policy was severely attacked by persons but with a superficial understanding of Tamil culture. 'Practices for which de Nobili had got permission from Rome were henceforth decided upon by people who had no knowledge of India'.[25]

Roberto de Nobili is a rare example of inculturation far in advance of his time. His adaptation was not superficial. It was not confined to externals such as dress and symbols, but represented a profound appreciation and appropriation of Tamil culture as a vehicle for Christian faith. In S. M. Michael's learned opinion, de Nobili so Tamilised Christianity that he touched the heart of Tamil culture. His adaptations enabled the Christians to retain their Tamil cultural identity. 'As a result, the converted Christians were not culturally alienated from the other non-Christian Tamilians'.[26]

Modern critics for methods designed to appeal to the Brahmins and other 'twice-born' castes have castigated De Nobili. We are wrong however to evaluate de Nobili from the vantage point of the twenty-first century. His initiatives toward the so-called higher castes were well intended as he regarded them as the essential means to penetrate India with the gospel. By his principles of adaptation he made the Christian message meaningful and acceptable, and thereby 'laid the foundation of a genuinely Indian Church by gathering around him some two hundred high caste neophytes and elaborating with them

24 Thomas Anchukandam, *Roberto de Nobili's Responsio (1610), A Vindication of Inculturation and Adaptation*, Bangalore: Kristu Jyoti Publications, 1996.

25 Elizabeth Koepping, 'India, Pakistan, Bangladesh, Burma/Myanmar' in *Christianities in Asia* edited by Peter C. Phan, Chichester, West Sussex, UK: Wiley-Blackwell, 2011, 18.

26 S. M. Michael, 'Catholic Mission in the Region of Tamilnadu' in *Integral Mission Dynamics: An Interdisciplinary Study of the Catholic Church in India* edited by Augustine Kanjamala, New Delhi: Intercultural Publications, 1995, 63.

his method of adaptation'.[27] Nobili's successors baptised some 5,000 new converts annually and reported a Christian community of more than 150,000 in the Madurai area, 'second only in numbers to that of Portuguese Goa'.[28] Moreover it is to be noted that most converts were from the lower castes who, it is evident, were not excluded by his approach.

Roberto de Nobili's greatest contribution was in his scholarship. The author of more than twenty books in the Tamil language, he is regarded as the father of Tamil prose,[29] and has been honoured for his contribution to Tamil culture. His accurate knowledge of the people, his fluency in speech and writing, opened an approach to the Tamil people and simultaneously opened the Tamils to the larger world beyond. De Nobili gave a terminology for Christian theology, a vehicle for conveying Christian ideas. Achievements of de Nobili were indeed 'Noble' and many, his success among the higher castes 'almost unparalleled'.[30]

## John De Britto & Constantine Joseph Beschi

Two other Jesuits of distinction in the Tamil country were John de Britto (1647-1693) who came to India in 1673 and Constantine Joseph Beschi (1680-1747) who served in the mission from 1711 to 1742. De Britto served among the Maravas of Ramnad and in Pudukottah. Considerable advance was followed by a period of persecution during which no Jesuit was permitted. De Britto's first visit in 1686 together with six companions ended in their arrest and torture. Eventually all were set free, but de Britto was forbidden by the Raja to preach Christianity in the land of the Maravas. In 1691, Britto was able to re-enter Marava Nadu where he not only preached but baptised several Marava converts. As a result, Britto was arrested

27 Sauliére, *His Star in the East*, xxvi.

28 Moffett, *History of Christianity in Asia*, 22.

29 Joseph Thekkedath, *From the Middle of the Sixteenth Century to the End of the Seventeenth Century*, History of Christian in India Vol. II, Bangalore: Church History Association of India, 1988, 252.

30 Neill, *History of Christian Missions*, 187.

along with his companions and brought to Ramanathapuram where he and his companions were thrown into a common cell.[31] De Britto, whose devotion and gentleness 'had made a deep impression on Christians and Hindus alike', on 4 February 1693 was publicly beheaded, one of the few missionary martyrs of the Church in India.[32]

Constantine Joseph Beschi's extraordinary mastery of the Tamil language brought great fame in that his work has been compared to that of the great Hindu seers. Beschi's legacy included 'epics, philosophical treatises, commentaries, dictionaries, grammars, translations, and tracts for Hindu–Christians and non-Christians alike'.[33] A long Christian epic, the *Tembavani,* is regarded a minor classic of Tamil literature.[34]

## Joseph Vaz

From the Tamil country it is important to return briefly to Goa to realise the importance of that Portuguese colony for the spread of the Catholic Faith. The highly significant Joseph Vaz (1650-1711), Brahman convert and Roman Catholic missionary from Goa, is said to have saved the Catholic Church in Ceylon (Sri Lanka) from extinction. Ordained a priest in 1675, Vaz worked for three years as a missionary in Kanara (Mangalore). Returning to Goa in 1685, he joined a new community of native priests named the Oratorians, then secretly left for Sri Lanka where he entered disguised as a beggar. There he served among the suppressed underground Catholics until

31 Leonard Fernando, 'Britto, John de' in the *Oxford Encyclopaedia of South Asian Christianity*, edited by R. E. Hedlund, J. M. Athyal, J. Kalapati and Jessica Richard, New Delhi: Oxford University Press, 2012.

32 Neill, *History of Christian Missions*, 188.

33 Robert Eric Frykenberg, 'Beschi, Constanzo Guiseppe' in the *Oxford Encyclopaedia of South Asian Christianity*, edited by R. E. Hedlund, J. M. Athyal, J. Kalapati and Jessica Richard,New Delhi: Oxford University Press, 2012.

34 Neill, *History of Christian Missions*, 188.

his death. 'So successful was he that other Oratorians were sent to join him, and finally the churches could no longer be kept hidden'.[35]

Vaz trained a band of missionaries, created an administrative structure by dividing the mission territory into eight districts and stationing a priest at every centre, produced an indigenous liturgy, organised a lay leadership, and produced copious Catholic literature through the genius of his companion Fr Jacome Gonsalves. Through these means Vaz and his small band of Oratorians managed to recover 'what the missionaries had during the Portuguese rule' and indeed much more, as they made it a truly local (Sri Lankan) Church.[36]

The Goan missionary Joseph Vaz rightly deserves to be known as the 'Apostle of Ceylon/Sri Lanka'. Vaz was beatified by Pope John Paul II in Colombo on 21 January 1995 and canonised by Pope Francis on 14 January 2015 on the second day of Pope Francis' Apostolic visit to Sri Lanka as Sri Lanka's first Catholic saint. The canonisation Mass, which took place at Colombo's seafront Galle Face Green before a crowd of more than 500,000, was probably one of the biggest public gatherings the city has ever witnessed.[37]

## At the Court of Akbar the Great

Turning once again to exploits of the Jesuits in India, this time to the North, to Hindustan and the Moghul court of Akbar the Great at Agra. Akbar, described as one of the greatest monarchs in recorded history, was deeply interested in religion and philosophy. A devout orthodox Muslim, later in life he was influenced by Sufi mysticism. He also was an exceptionally tolerant ruler who pleased his Hindu subjects by abolishing the oppressive poll tax habitually imposed upon non-Muslims. Having heard of the activities of the

35 Moffett, *History of Christianity in Asia*, 227.

36 Don Alexis Dassanayake, 'Vaz, Joseph' in the *Oxford Encyclopaedia of South Asian Christianity*, edited by R. E. Hedlund, J. M. Athyal, J. Kalapati and Jessica Richard, New Delhi:Oxford University Press, 2012.

37 John Baptist Tumusiime, 'Pope Francis canonises St. Joseph Vaz, Sri Lanka's first saint', Vatican Radio, 14/01/2015 15:36, engafrica@vatiradio.va Accessed on 16 July 2015.

Jesuits, Akbar extended an invitation to the Jesuit headquarters in Goa requesting a mission to the imperial Moghul court.[38] Akbar appears to have wanted to know more about the religion that taught its followers about ethical obligations toward the State, perhaps also to obtain information about the political power behind the trade and military settlements along the western coast.[39] Goa speedily dispatched three Jesuit missionaries who reached the emperor's court at Fatehpur Sikri (near Agra) in 1579 where they were cordially received. Among them the aristocratic Rudolph Acquaviva appears to have most impressed Akbar. Hopes ran high for the conversion of Akbar and other members of his court, but this was not to be, and the three returned to Goa. A second request was given in 1590, and again Goa sent three missionaries who returned after a few months. A third mission at the request of Akbar was sent in 1594, lead by the grandnephew of Francis Xavier, Jerome Xavier who created Christian literature in Persian and developed a method of public debate with the Hindus and Muslims. This third mission lasted for a couple of centuries until the suppression of the Jesuits by the Pope. The Jesuit missionaries learned Persian (the court language), wrote books, saw a few conversions and provided pastoral care to Armenian Catholics and others living in north India.[40]

Perhaps the mission to Akbar was based on a miscalculation—that at least is the conclusion of historian Stephen Neill.[41] Akbar had become dissatisfied with orthodox Islam, and for a time at least he encouraged a form of dialogue or disputation in which Islamic scholars together with other religions would debate various issues. Participants in these public meetings included Hindus, Muslims,

38 Moffett, *History of Christianity in Asia*, 23-24.

39 George Gispert-Sauch, 'Jesuit Mission to the Mughal Court' in the *Oxford Encyclopaedia of South Asian Christianity*, edited by R. E. Hedlund, J. M. Athyal, J. Kalapati and Jessica Richard, New Delhi: Oxford University Press, 2012, 352.

40 George Gispert-Sauch, 'Xavier, Jerome' in the *Oxford Encyclopaedia of South Asian Christianity*, edited by R. E. Hedlund, J. M. Athyal, J. Kalapati and Jessica Richard, New Delhi: Oxford University Press, 2012, 749.

41 Neill, *History of Christian Missions*, 152.

Christians, Parsees, Jains, Jews and even atheists states Amartya Sen.[42] This did not mean that Akbar was ready to convert. To the contrary, Akbar was evaluating the virtues of the various religions in order to create a new religion incorporating the merits of them all. The *Din Illahi* was proclaimed just at the time of the arrival at the court of the first Jesuit mission. The new religion never really took root, and rapidly faded away after the death of Akbar. Its importance, states Neill, is that 'it closed the mind of Akbar to any serious considerations of the Christian faith'.[43] Nevertheless, Akbar continued to permit Christian preaching and public conversion, and by 1598 there were at least four churches in his realm at Agra and Lahore and possibly at Cambay and Thatta.[44]

None of Akbar's successors displayed the same degree of toleration. Nevertheless there were some lasting effects of the Jesuit mission to Emperor Akbar's court, particularly in the arts. 'The flourishing of Mughal art, especially painting, was greatly influenced by Christian models, which found their way to north India through the missionaries'.[45]

42 Amartya Sen, *The Argumentative Indian: Writings on Indian Culture, History and Identity*, London, New York, New Delhi: Penguin Books, 2005, 18.

43 Neill, *History of Christian Missions*, 153.

44 Moffett, *History of Christianity in Asia*, 24.

45 George Gispert-Sauch, 'Jesuit Mission to the Mughal Court' in the *Oxford Encyclopaedia of South Asian Christianity*, edited by R. E. Hedlund, J. M. Athyal, J. Kalapati and Jessica Richard, New Delhi: Oxford University Press, 2012, 352.

Chapter 4

# And Then the Protestants Came
## Pietists, Baptists & Others

From the beginnings of Apostolic Christianity in India and its developments during the early centuries of the era, we caught glimpses of Indian Christianity during the seemingly 'silent' years of the Middle Ages until the advent of the Portuguese explorers at the beginning of the modern era. Indian Christianity would never be the same. The newcomers were pleasantly surprised to discover the existence of an ancient body of believers whose resilient faith was clearly Christian yet differed in liturgy and some other points from the European Christendom of the Portuguese. Inevitably there were tensions and discord as Catholic Christianity found a place in the subcontinent. Alternative versions of Christianity including the Nestorians and other 'Eastern' expressions of the Faith also found their way to India where they interacted with the existing Thomas Christianity. But there was more to come.

## Pietist Protestants

The European Protestant Reformation of the sixteenth century did not immediately gave birth to a missionary movement. Various explanations have been offered – the Protestants fighting for their lives (against the Catholics) could give no thought to mission; Protestants fighting Protestants (controversies and heresies) consumed their zeal; geographical restrictions (Spain and Portugal controlled the trade routes); psychological limitation of dependency upon the ruler to provide for the spiritual needs of his subjects (territorial concept of the Church).[1] Whatever the reasons, with a few small exceptions, the Reformers did not engage in mission beyond the borders of Christendom. It is not that the Reformers were unaware of the non-Christian world. Luther for example had considerable to say about the Jews and the Turks.[2] Calvin is believed to have encouraged the launch of a mission to South America.[3] King Gustava Vasa of Sweden encouraged mission among the Lapps of northern Scandinavia.[4] Protestant missionary animation however was to come from the margins of the Reformation, from 'radical' groups, Pietists, Moravians and Anabaptists. Through the agency of such groups Protestant Christianity came to India.

Pietism has been defined as a reformation movement within established Protestantism, especially the Lutheran Church of Germany in which Philip Jacob Spener (1635-1705) was the reformer. Pietism was a reformation of Christian life with emphasis on heart-felt religion, conversion, personal holiness, spiritual priesthood of believers, and activation of the laity.[5] Pietism also

1 Stephen Neill, *A History of Christian Missions*, Baltimore: Penguin Books, 1964, 220-21.

2 Ibid., 222.

3 [Documentation is found in a thesis by a Korean scholar and in a journal article not accessible to me at present.]

4 Stephen Neill, *A History of Christian Missions*, 223.

5 Theodore G. Tappert, 'Introduction' to *Pia Desideria* by Philip Jacob Spener, Translated and edited by Theodore G. Tappert, Philadelphia: Fortress Press, 1964, 19.

was known as a 'church within the Church' derived from Spener's practice of conducting private meetings 'for the cultivation of holiness' consisting of prayer, discussion of the previous Sunday's sermon, readings from a devotional book or Bible study. Church renewal was to come through 'the remnant of true Christians in every congregation'.[6] Spener's book, *Pia Desideria* became a tool for the worldwide spread of this spiritual movement. Spener's successor, August Herman Francke (1663-1727), was given an appointment in the new University of Halle, which was to have a significant role in dispatching the first Protestant missionaries to India.

## Tranquebar and Ziegenbalg

It happened this way: King Frederick IV of Denmark, desiring to deploy missionaries to his Indian subjects in the tiny Danish colony of Tranquebar on the south-east Indian coast, was unable to find suitable candidates from Denmark, therefore appealed to the Pietist centre at Halle University in Germany. There August Hermann Francke quickly supplied two young men, Bartholomew Ziegenbalg and Henry Plütschau, who sailed from Europe in late 1705 and arrived at Tranquebar on 9 July 1706, under the Royal Danish-Halle Mission, 'the first non-Roman Catholic missionaries to reach India from Europe'.[7] Initial hostility and harassment by the Danish community and governor had to be overcome. Gradually, the missionaries overcame the obstacles and were able to begin their work. Ziegenbalg was a devoted scholar who mastered the Tamil language, translated the New Testament and part of the Old into Tamil [said to be the first Bible translation into any Indian language], wrote books, produced a Tamil-German dictionary among other works initiating the production of Tamil Christian literature. Ziegenbalg and the early German missionaries adapted their Pietist (Halle) educational

6 Theodore G. Tappert, 'Introduction' to *Pia Desideria* by Philip Jacob Spener, Translated and edited by Theodore G. Tappert, Philadelphia: Fortress Press, 1964, 13, 19, 22.

7 Stephen Neill, *A History of Christian Missions*, Baltimore: Penguin Books, 1964, 228.

tradition to the formation of Christian faith and character in Tamilnadu.[8] Ziegenbalg was a pioneer in the Western study of South Indian culture.[9] The translation project was a joint effort between missionaries with knowledge of the biblical Greek and Hebrew and the Tamils who knew their own language and culture. Translation of the Bible into Tamil laid the foundation for an indigenous Church in India.[10] 'From the beginning, Ziegenbalg appears to have grasped the principle of *inculturation*, developing an indigenous church with Indian characteristics in architecture, music, caste, and customs'.[11]

Five principles emerge from the Pietist mission:

1. Church and school must go together. Converts must be able to read the Word of God; therefore all Christian children must be educated.
2. In order to read the Bible, the Word must be available to the Christians in their own language. For this to happen, Ziegenbalg set to work translating first the New Testament, then the Old, and had progressed up to the Book of Ruth before his death. This was completed by Johann Philipp Fabricius whose entire Bible appeared in 1796.
3. Preaching must be based on an accurate knowledge of the beliefs and culture of the people. Ziegenbalg made a careful study of the beliefs of the people, which he sent to Europe for publication—for which he received a rebuke that his role was to root out Hinduism in India, not propagate heathen superstition in Europe.
4. They must aim for definite, personal conversion.

8 Hugald Grafe, *The History of Christianity in Tamilnadu*, History of Christianity in India Vol. 4, Part 2; Bangalore: Church History Association of India, 1982, 188.

9 Hans-Werner Gensichen, 'Ziegenbalg, Bartholmäus' in the *Biographical Dictionary of Christian Missions* edited by Gerald H. Anderson, New York: Simon & Schuster Macmillan, 1997, 761-2.

10 Daniel Jeyaraj, 'Early Tamil Bible Translation in Tranquebar', *Dharma Deepika* June 1997, 75.

11 James A. Scherer, 'Bartholomew Ziegenbalg', *Missiology* October 1999, 493.

5. As early as possible an Indian Church must come into being with its own Indian ministry.[12]

Sound principles and good intentions not withstanding, it was only in 1728 that the mission board in Denmark, with the King's approval, granted the missionaries in India the authority to ordain Indian Christians.[13] The first person chosen was Aaron. Aaron, whose Hindu name was Arumugam, came to faith in Christ, and was baptised by Ziegenbalg on 5 August, 1718. Ziegenbalg gave him the name Aaron, which was the name of the first priest in Israel. After pastoral training, Aaron was ordained according to the Danish Lutheran rite on 28 December, 1733 in the New Jerusalem Church in Tranquebar.[14]

> His ordination strengthened the Christians in the countryside and encouraged many non-Christians to approach him without shame or fear. Whenever there were troubles between Christians and non-Christians his status as a priest helped him to solve the problems. The missionaries realized that the ordination of Aaron opened a new era in the history of the Indian Church.[15]

## Rajanaikan

Growth and extension of the Church into new territories, however, was not dependent upon ordained clergy. The unexpected arrival of one Rajanaikan, a zealous Christian layman from across the Tanjore

12 Stephen Neill, *A History of Christian Missions*, Baltimore: Penguin Books, 1964, 229-30.

13 Samuel H. Moffett, *A History of Christianity in Asia: Vol. II, 1500-1900*, Maryknoll: Orbis Books, 2005, 240.

14 Eva Maria Siebert–Johnson, 'Aaron, the First Ordained Protestant Indian Pastor' in the *Oxford Encyclopaedia of South Asian Christianity*, edited by R.E. Hedlund, J. M. Athyal, J. Kalapati and Jessica Richard, New Delhi: Oxford University Press, 2011.

15 Daniel Jeyaraj, 'Dual Identity of Christians in Tranquebar', *Dharma Deepika*, December 1997, 16.

border, provided the possibility of outreach into Indian Territory beyond the scope of the European missionaries. The return of Rajanaikan, a former Catholic, now a Lutheran evangelist, provoked a violent confrontation between Catholics and Protestants in which Rajanaikan's father was killed and two brothers wounded. 'But the Lutherans kept coming and growing. In the next ten years Rajanaikan had tripled the number of Protestants in Tanjore'.[16]

Rajanaikan's successor was a missionary who ranks, along with Ziegenbalg, as the greatest of the German Pietists in India, Christian Friedrich Schwarz (1726-1798), who came to Tranquebar in 1750 and remained in India for half a century until his death in 1798. Within four months he was preaching in Tamil, and in his second year he baptised four hundred converts whom he had instructed in the Faith.[17] Schwartz built upon the work of Ziegenbalg in laying the foundation for what became 'the largest and strongest evangelical Christian community in India'.[18] As Frykenberg points out, even before Schwartz arrived in India 'an evangelical form of Tamil Christianity had already gained a firm foothold in South India'.[19] After fifteen years in Tranquebar Schwarz moved to Trichinopoly where he engaged in ministry to Muslims for which he learned both Hindustani and Persian. During this period, Schwarz was supported by the Society for the Promotion of Christian Knowledge (SPCK). The last twenty years of his life were spent in Tanjore (Thanjavur) as the 'Raja-Guru' of the young prince, Serfoji Maharaja, and as mentor of Vedanayagam Sastri, future 'poet laureate' of Thanjavur whose works would serve to launch modern Tamil literature.[20]

---

16 Samuel H. Moffett, *A History of Christianity in Asia: Vol. II, 1500-1900*, Maryknoll: Orbis Books, 2005, 241.

17 Ibid., 242.

18 Robert Eric Frykenberg, 'The Legacy of Christian Friedrich Schwartz', *International Bulletin of Missionary Research* July 1999, 132.

19 Ibid., 130.

20 Robert Eric Frykenberg, 'Christianity in South India Since 1500: Historical Studies of Transcultural Interactions within Hindu-Muslim Environments', *Dharma Deepika,* December 1997, 4.

Pietism had challenged the nominal Christianity of the official Lutheran Churches of Europe, awakening Lutherans to the need to engage in sending mission, all of which led to the founding of the Royal Danish Halle Mission — although formation in Britain of the Society for Promoting Christian Knowledge (SPCK, 1698) and the Society for the Propagation of the Gospel in Foreign Parts (SPG, 1701) also provided indirect influence.[21] News reports from the Tranquebar Mission also had a profound impact upon the emerging Protestant missionary movement and helped leaders in the West to expand their understanding of cross-cultural mission.[22] More important is the fact that, as Dana Robert observes, indigenous converts 'remade missionary Christianity into their own images'.[23]

## The Moravians

Closely akin to the Pietists were the Moravians, also known as the Bohemian Brethren (*Unitas Fratrum*), spiritual descendants of the fifteenth century reformer John Hus. Exiled from Moravia, the persecuted Hussites were given shelter by Count Nicolaus Ludwig von Zinzendorf on his estate at Herrnhut. Zinzendorf organised the refugees into a Church which developed its own distinctive pietism centered in a passionate devotion to Christ the crucified Redeemer and a radical call for total surrender to the Saviour's will. 'Under the leadership of Zinzendorf this small Church was seized with a missionary passion which has never left it'. Moravian missionaries tended to be laypersons, skilled artisans, tradesmen and peasants who aimed to 'live the Gospel, and so to commend it to those who

21 Daniel Jeyaraj, 'Mission Reports from South India and Their Impact on the Western Mind: The Tranquebar Mission of the Eighteenth Century' in *Converting Colonialism: Visions and Realities in Mission History, 1706-1914*, edited by Dana L. Robert, Grand Rapids & Cambridge: Eerdmans Publishing, 2008, 22.

22 Ibid., 41.

23 Dana L. Robert (ed.), *Converting Colonialism: Visions and Realities in Mission History, 1706-1914*, Grand Rapids & Cambridge: Eerdmans Publishing, 2008, 20.

have never heard it'.[24] 'Heart-religion' was the main qualification for missionary service. Initially there was no formal training, but missionaries were encouraged 'to work at a trade and to itinerate as much as possible'.[25] Zinzendorf trained his congregation 'through an apprenticeship model, mentoring his workers via letters and instructions, and visiting the mission settlements'. Zinzendorf was a scholar who favoured academic training, and eventually formal educational institutions also were formed. By 1760, the year of Zinzendorf's death, the Moravian Church had sent out at least 226 missionaries, more than half the Protestant missionaries sent from Europe in the eighteenth century.[26]

Moravian missionaries first arrived in India at Tranquebar in 1760 enroute to the Nicobar Islands. They were not well received in Tranquebar but were treated by the Danish Mission as intruders rather than allies. The enthusiastic unordained Tamil evangelist Rajanaikan, on the other hand, 'found in the Moravians a kindred zeal and worked with them most closely'.[27] The Moravian mission to the Nicobars lasted for twenty years, but ended in apparent failure with the death of the missionaries. A mission in 1777 to Serampore near Calcutta lasted fifteen years during which a number of Bengali translations were produced, but due to 'lack of cooperation by the authorities' was abandoned prior to the arrival of William Carey who found little trace of their work in Serampore.[28]

The Moravians generally did not plant new churches but rather formed small cells for Bible study, prayer and evangelism to enrich the spirituality of existing congregations.[29] But there were exceptions,

---

24 Stephen Neill, *A History of Christian Missions*, Baltimore: Penguin Books, 1964, 237.

25 Robert L. Gallagher, 'Zinzendorf and the Early Moravians: Pioneers in Leadership Selection and Training',*Missiology: An InternationalReview*, XXXVI, 2, April 2008: 237-244, 239.

26 Gallagher, 'Zinzendorf and the Early Moravians', 242-3.

27 Moffett, *History of Christianity in Asia*, 243.

28 Ibid., 243-4.

29 Ibid., 243.

e.g., in Ladakh where the pioneering Moravians, in the absence of any other Christians, created a Moravian Church which still exists and carries on an active witness.[30] The Moravian Church in the Ladakh region goes back to the 1860s and the visit of the young Moravian missionary August Wilhelm Heyde. In August 1885, the Rev. Redslob moved to Ladakh as the first resident missionary, and in January 1887 a small school was started in the Leh bazaar. Today, the Moravian Mission School stands as the largest and one of the best academic institutions in the Ladakh region.[31]

## Colonial Opposition

The work of the Pietist, Moravian and other early Protestant missions described in this chapter took place during the colonial era. The point is important given that not infrequently it is assumed that the development of Christianity in India was tied to colonialism, whereas in actuality colonialism impeded the work of the missions. The altruistic objectives of the missionaries clashed with the mercenary goals of the colonialists. With reference to the Danish colonialists at Tranquebar, historian Stephen Neill states that 'Colonialism wished to have nothing whatever to do with missions'.[32] As the British expanded their Empire in India, they sometimes found the missionaries 'useful' for some particular chore, but nevertheless an official 'unfriendliness towards missions' continued as long as the British ruled India.[33] Frykenberg refers to the Pietist/Evangelical missionaries of the eighteenth century in India as 'pre-colonial' or 'anti-colonial' whose literary and scholarly contributions were

30 See Elijah Gergan, 'Archives: Moravian Church Library, Leh, Ladakh' in the *Oxford Encyclopaedia of South Asian Christianity*, edited by R. E. Hedlund, J. M. Athyal, J. Kalapati and Jessica Richard, New Delhi:Oxford University Press, 2012.

31 V. S. J. Dogar, 'Jammu and Kashmir' in the*Oxford Encyclopaedia of South Asian Christianity*, edited by R. E. Hedlund, J. M. Athyal, J. Kalapati and Jessica Richard, New Delhi: Oxford University Press, 2012.

32 Stephen Neill, *Colonialism and Christian Missions*. New York: McGraw-Hill, 1966, 77.

33 Ibid., 99.

devoted to the welfare of the Indian people.[34] In her stimulating edited collection with the provocative title *Converting Colonialism*, Dana Robert comments about the importance of the Pietist mission to India as 'unsurpassed in the annals of early Protestant missions'. She further states, 'Their combination of translation into the local language and the founding of schools and social services set a pattern that nearly all future Protestant missions followed. Their ambiguous relationship with colonial power...also foreshadowed nineteenth-century trends'.[35]

Ambiguity (or indifference and sometimes hostility) very well describes the attitude of the British East India Company (EIC) toward Christian missions. As we have noted, colonialism was not conducive to missionary activity, but missions were tolerated by the EIC when providing needed religious services to British inhabitants in British India.[36]

## Chaplains: Henry Martyn and John Kiernander

Relatively few missionaries were permitted in North India. Despite this antipathy, the EIC did find a place for chaplains if for no other reason than to conduct funerals and to provide for the religious needs of the several hundred Europeans residing in Calcutta (Kolkata). Among them were several 'pious' chaplains who also rendered exceptional service to the local Indian population. Best known was the brilliant Cambridge scholar and Anglican evangelical, Henry Martyn, who arrived in India in 1806 and devoted his life to the Muslims. By the time of his death 12 years later, Martyn had translated the entire Bible into Urdu and the New Testament into

34 Robert Eric Frykenberg, *Christianity in India: From Beginnings to the Present*, New York: Oxford University Press, 2008, 153.

35 Dana Robert, *Converting Colonialism*, 7-8.

36 Andrew Porter, *Religion versus empire? British Protestant missionaries and overseas expansion, 1700-1914*, Manchester & New York: Manchester University Press, 2004, 64, 68.Carey and other missionaries earned goodwill by their behaviour and their service rendered at Fort William College (69).

Persian.[37] It has been said that Martyn did more for the cause of missions than almost any other missionary in modern times.[38]

Another chaplain, less well-known but of considerable importance, was the Swedish Pietist John Zachary Kiernander (1710-1798), educated at Uppsala and Halle, sent to India under the Danish-Halle Mission where he served first at Tranquebar, then at Calcutta, said to be the first Protestant missionary in Bengal.[39] Kiernander and two Indian assistants were sent to Calcutta from Tranquebar under the Anglican Society for the Propagation of the Gospel (SPG), with partial support from the Danish-Halle Mission at Tranquebar. This is an interesting case of collaboration involving three missions — the Royal Danish Mission, the SPG and the SPCK — in a common cause. Trained at Halle and sent to India by the SPG, Kiernander was 'more missionary than chaplain'. At Calcutta Kiernander moved beyond the commercial and military establishment and began a ministry to local Eurasians and Bengalis. He also built a church (founded in 1770) on his own property and named it 'The House of Prayer'. Later it was renamed the 'Old Mission Church' by the Anglican chaplains, which name it bears still today.[40] In 1787, Kiernander became bankrupt due to some indiscrete investments by his son, and the Old Mission Church was put to auction but was purchased by Charles Grant who transferred the property to the SPCK. The Old Mission Church served as a centre for evangelical activity. It was here that EIC Chaplain David Brown preached most of his sermons, its services attracting so many leaders of Calcutta that the facility had to be enlarged.[41]

37 Moffett, *History of Christianity in Asia*, 264.

38 Eyre Chatterton, *A History of the Church of England in India: Since the Early Days of the East India Company*, Chapter VII, 'The Evangelical Chaplains, 1787-1815', London: SPCK, 1924. Available at: http://www.google.com/search?hl=en&source=hp&biw=899&bih=810 [Accessed on 3rd November, 2011, 8:04 PM].

39 K. P. Sen Gupta, *The Christian Missionaries in Bengal 1793-1833*, Calcutta: Firma K. L. Mukhopadhyay, 1971, 17.

40 Moffett, *History of Christianity in Asia*, 245.

41 Chatterton, *History of the Church of England in India*, 3.

## Calcutta

During this era the centre of Protestant missionary activity shifted from Tranquebar to Calcutta.[42] Because the missionaries tended to attack prevailing social evils, it is helpful to review a description of social conditions of Bengal in the eighteenth century by Bengali historian, K. P. Sen Gupta. The most important feature of Hinduism was the worship of innumerable gods and goddesses as well as numerous religious festivals of which Durga Puja was the national festival in Bengal. Another major festival was the Charak-puja in honour of Shiva during which devotees engaged in self-tortures such as the infamous hook-swinging ritual in which volunteers (always lower caste) were suspended by a hook attached to the flesh of their backs while being swung in a circle around a pole.[43] Other popular deities were the goddesses of diseases such as smallpox, cholera, and snakes. Every village or town had its own guardian deity believed responsible for the welfare of the community. Other objects of popular worship were the sun, moon, River Ganges, the Pipal tree and the Tulsi plant. Practices deemed abhorrent included *sati* (voluntary widow burning) and the custom on certain auspicious days at the mouth of the Ganges River to throw the first-born baby into the sea.[44] These and other horrendous acts documented by eye-witnesses and reported by Baptist missionary William Ward included voluntary suicide, drowning in the Ganges, burning of lepers, burial alive, infanticide, various forms of self-murder.[45] Everyday life was dominated by caste rules, which regulated every aspect of life from birth to death. 'These rules were strictly enforced by the

42 Moffett, *History of Christianity in Asia*, 244.

43 Sen Gupta, *Christian Missionaries in Bengal*, 22. Also see Geoffrey A. Oddie, *Popular Religion, Elites, and Reform: Hook-Swinging and its Prohibition in Colonial India, 1800-1894*, New Delhi: Manohar, 1995.

44 Sen Gupta, *Christian Missionaries in Bengal*, 22, 23.

45 William Ward, *History, Literature, and Mythology of the Hindus*, Vol. IV, First Published 1817-1820, Third Edition (Abridged & Improved), Delhi: Low Price Publication, 1990 Reprint, 96-125.

Brahmans who reigned supreme in Hindu Society'.[46] The Hindus believed that all religions were but different ways to reach God; therefore 'everyone should seek salvation through his own religion'. Bengali Muslims tended to join with the Hindus in celebrating Hindu festivals and paying homage to Hindu deities.[47] Hindus also participated in Muslim festivals and in 'Pir' worship.[48] There was no clear distinction between the two religions.

This, states Sen Gupta, was the background against which the missionaries had to work when William Carey and John Thomas arrived in Bengal in 1793.[49]

46 Sen Gupta, *Christian Missionaries in Bengal*, 23.

47 Ibid., 22-23, 25.

48 'Pirs' were Muslim saints whose tombs had become shrines for popular devotion, for which there was no sanction in the Qu'ran.

49 Sen Gupta, *Christian Missionaries in Bengal*, 29.

Chapter 5

# Christian Identity, Distortions and More

When Carey and the first Baptist missionaries arrived in Bengal in 1793 they were neophytes, pioneers with comparatively little precedence for their venture. Carey however had made a careful study of the few sources available leading to publication of a document, which has been classed among the founding documents of the modern Protestant missionary movement.[1] More important it launched the formation of the Baptist Missionary Society, which sent Carey and John Thomas to India. In his missionary apologetic Carey made particular reference to the missionary activities of the Moravians as well as to the work of David Brainerd among aboriginal tribes in North America, and to B. Ziegenbalg and C. F. Schwartz at Tranquebar in South India.

1 William Carey, *An Enquiry into the Obligations of Christians to use Means for the Conversion of the Heathens*, Leicester: Ann Ireland, and other Booksellers, 1792.

## William Carey

Carey, at least in the Protestant world, is an *icon*. In common with other legendary figures, Carey has been mythologised. If so, demythologising will be in order. Carey was a child of the Enlightenment, a point made clear in other studies. That in itself, however, does not define the person of Carey. His poverty and working class origins likewise were formative aspects during his life in England, but not the whole story. More significant than any other influence was Carey's evangelical faith. His religious experience motivated his provocative suggestion that Baptists in England consider the appropriateness of positive response to the missionary commission of the New Testament. The implications of that question led to publication of Carey's *Enquiry* as well as to formation of the Baptist Missionary Society and to Carey's departure to India.

Carey's evangelicalism did not arise in a vacuum. There were several centuries of precedents including Lutheran Pietism[2] in Germany and Scandinavia, Zinzendorf and the Moravians[3], Anabaptist radicalism and the Believers' Church tradition[4] (of which

---

2 Philip Jacob Spener, *Pia Desideria*, translated, edited, and with an introduction by Theodore G. Tappert. Philadelphia: Fortress Press, 1964. Also see Carter Lindberg, ed. *The Pietist Theologians: An Introduction to Theology in the Seventeenth & Eighteenth Centuries.* Malden, MA, & Oxford, UK: Blackwell Publishing, 2005.

3 Peter Vogt, 'Nicholas Ludwig von Zinzendorf (1700-1760)' in Carter Lindberg, ed. *The Pietist Theologians,* Also see W.R. Ward, *The Protestant Evangelical Awakening,* Cambridge University Press, 1982; and Robert L. Gallagher, 'Zinzendorf and the Early Moravians: Pioneers in Leadership Selection and Training'. *Missiology: An International Review*, XXXVI, 2 April 2008.

4 Donald F. Durnbaugh, *The Believers' Church: The History and Character of Radical Protestantism*, New York: Macmillan, 1968. Also see John D. Roth, 'An Anabaptist Church: A Third Way Emerges' in *Stories: How Mennonites Came to Be,* Scottdale: Herald Press, 2008, 65-85.

the English Baptists were a part), the Wesleyan revival and the theology of Jonathan Edwards and George Whitefield.[5]

In planning their mission methodology, Carey and the BMS missionaries followed the example of the Moravians. They concentrated on three activities: 1) learning the language of the people, 2) translating Scripture into the regional language, and 3) starting vernacular elementary schools.[6] Inevitably there was much more. Carey and Serampore identified with the daily struggles of the people. Colonial harassment and antagonism to the Serampore Mission is one component of the story. Missionary intervention and exposure of colonial exploitation of the inhabitants of India is another. Mission history must be de-colonialised, as Dharmaraj insists.[7] It would be a mistake to subsume all mission history as part of colonial history or to hypothesise mission history as a mere appendage of colonial history. There is no escaping the fact that Western colonialism made mission possible (at least in some of the forms known in the modern era) beyond the West. Christian mission has been tainted by this unfortunate colonial alignment. Generalisations, however, are dangerous. True in part, but not in full, viz., the case in point. Initially Carey and his colleagues were victims of colonial oppression and only later to some extent its beneficiaries. It is an unfortunate distortion to completely categorise the missionary movement together with colonisation.[8] History records the active opposition of Carey and his associates, as well as other notable missionaries,[9] to the

5 Kenneth Hylson-Smith, *To the Ends of the Earth: The Globalization of Christianity*. London: Paternoster, 2007, 23-30.

6 K. P. Sen Gupta, *The Christian Missionaries in Bengal 1793-1833*, Calcutta: Firma K.L. Mukhopadhyay, 1971, 32-33.

7 Jacob S. Dharmaraj, *Colonialism and Christian Mission: Postcolonial Reflections*, Delhi: ISPCK,1993.

8 See the review of Dharmaraj's book by F. Hrangkhuma, *Dharma Deepika*, December 1995, 86-87.

9 For example missionary Long of the London Missionary Society who fought for 30 years on behalf of the oppressed subjects of rural Bengal and opposed the colonial regime. See Abhijit Dutta, *Christian Missionaries on the Indigo Question in Bengal*, Calcutta: Minerva, 1989.

structures of colonialism. In various ways, Carey and the Serampore missionaries identified with the daily struggles of the people.

## Serampore

Carey had a passion for developing the languages of India including the preservation of Sanskrit. Serampore birthed a linguistic renaissance in India.[10] As early as 1804 Carey delivered a public lecture in Sanskrit at Fort William College. In 1806, he composed a Sanskrit Grammar for student use. Later followed a six-volume Sanskrit Dictionary (which was destroyed in the disastrous 1812 Serampore fire) and an unpublished polyglot vocabulary. The entire Bible was translated by Carey into Sanskrit.

When Serampore College was founded in 1818, Sanskrit was made a compulsory subject. The Library of the College contained fourteen Sanskrit books and sixty-five Sanskrit manuscripts for use by its students and teachers.[11] At Serampore College Sanskrit was required, and English was permitted, but Bengali was prerequisite for all further study.[12] It is said that Bengali is closer to Sanskrit than is true of any other modern Indian language.[13]

While Sanskrit was important for classical studies, Serampore promoted the vernacular as the medium of instruction. In doing so they struck a *via media* between the Orientalists who wanted study of Sanskrit classics for the perpetuation of the classical tradition and the Anglicists who wanted Western education in English. Over a hundred schools were organised throughout Bengal, and many English books were translated into Bengali in order to provide 'modern' education in the local vernacular. Vernacular education was

---

10 S. K. Chatterjee, 'William Carey and the Linguistic Renaissance in India', 157-175.

11 Indira Mukhopadhayay, 'William Carey's Contributions for the Promotion of Sanskritic Studies' in *Carey's Obligation and India's Renaissance* edited by J. T. K. Daniel and R. E. Hedlund, 1993, 193-201.

12 Ibid., 199.

13 Kalidas Nag, 'Carey's Contribution to Bengali Literature' in *The Story of Serampore and Its College*, 100.

a distinct Serampore contribution to cultural revitalisation among the common people in modern India. Serampore and Carey in a number of ways contributed to cultural renewal.

## Transformation or Exploitation?

In North East India Christianity has been an effective catalyst for cultural renewal and social integration especially through education and developmental work. The Church, as seen by Christians, has been both an agent of change and a means of enforcing traditional values as well as filling voids, as is pointed out by several scholars. But there is a flipside – the alleged Christian exploitation of tribes and the erosion of culture, religion, and traditions. Critics tend to repeat this charge, which is conceded by local Christians to be at best a partial truth, at worst a gross distortion. In point of fact, Christianity has been a major source of moral, social and cultural transformation among the peoples of North East India.

Apart from the dominant Christianised peoples of the North East, India's marginalised *adivasis* (aboriginal tribes) present quite a different picture. These exploited peoples regarded the land and its forests and resources as the gifts of God to the original inhabitants of Central India's tribal belt. Unfortunately, there is a general tendency to view India's *adivasis* as 'primitives' and out-of-step with modernity. According to activist G. N. Devy, the tragic result is that the tribes remain 'trapped in the debris of colonial history' whereas 'there is much in the adivasi way of life that the country needs to emulate'.[14] Against the devastating effects of deprivation of tribal rights, Christianity gave the tribals a new identity and sense of dignity. Christian missionaries gave a written form to tribal languages, provided modern education, and helped the tribals fight legal battles to preserve their land rights.[15] Christianity has been a

14 G. N. Devy, *A Nomad Called Thief: Reflections on Adivasi Silence*, Hyderabad: Orient Longman, 2006, 11.

15 Nirmal Minz, 'Religion, Culture and Education in the Context of Tribal Aspirations in India' in *Little Traditions and National Culture,* edited by Thomas Kadankavil, 128.

major sustaining force for India's original inhabitants in their struggle against cultural attacks and empowering them for social-economic liberation.

## Conversion Repurcussions

In Bengal conversions were relatively few and accompanied by severe repurcussions. 'Not only the convert but his whole family was excommunicated'. In a few extreme cases converts were murdered. Others were socially ostracised to the extent that life became intolerable. 'No professional class would render them any service, landlords refused to recognise them as tenants'.[16] An attempted solution to form new villages for the converts was to some extent successful, but harassment continued throughout the period. Conversions created a violent reaction, which gradually subsided but was followed by enforcement of caste laws, which isolated the converts from society and application of the Hindu law of Inheritance by which the convert was denied any right to paternal property. The experience was much the same for all the Protestant missions: few converts, the majority from the lowest strata consisting of outcastes, half-castes and beggars.[17] The Christian mission in Bengal to all appearances was a failure. But there was more.

The Serampore missionaries, after years of deliberation, in 1818 issued a prospectus for a college in which Christians and non-Christians would study side by side. A 'theological institute' would be located in a college of arts and sciences 'because that alone would put future leaders of the Church in dialogue with the Indian and European cultures and develop a concern for the transformation of culture and equip them to communicate the gospel to the cultured'.[18] The Serampore missionaries gave importance to Oriental languages, particularly Sanskrit which they believed would give Indian Christians

16 Sen Gupta, *The Christian Missionaries in Bengal*, 159, 162.

17 Ibid., 159, 163-164.

18 M. M. Thomas, 'Carey's Vision of the Gospel, Its Relevance in India Today' in *Carey's Obligation and India's Renaissance*, edited by J. T. K. Daniel and R. E. Hedlund, Serampore: Council of Serampore College, 1993, 351.

a respected status among their countrymen. 'The Indian students both Christian and non-Christian were taught Sanskrit, Bengali, English and other useful knowledge'.[19]

The arrival of Alexander Duff from Scotland brought quite a different approach. Duff's plan was 'to make Christianity a self-developing power. This he hoped to achieve by educating and converting the members of the higher classes who in turn would convert their fellow countrymen'.[20] The medium of instruction would be English.

## Ram Mohan Roy

Although converts were few, the work of the missionaries had considerable impact on Bengali society. In their attack on *Sati* the missionaries were joined by Hindu reformers. Ram Mohan Roy published two tracts showing that the practice of *Sati* is nowhere sanctioned in the Hindu scriptures. When *Sati* was officially abolished (on 4 December 1829), upper caste orthodox Hindus were enraged and protested, whereas Ram Mohan Roy together with the missionaries was delighted and Roy congratulated the Governor-General on the abolition of the cruel rite.[21]

As a reformer, Roy also inveighed against polytheism and idolatry. The missionaries approved of Roy's activities, finding in Roy an ally and a potential convert to Christianity--wishful thinking and premature. Roy's intention was 'to introduce simple truths of Christianity to his countrymen in such a form that they could understand them', but, to the disappointment of the missionaries, Roy rejected the Christian doctrine of the Trinity as well as the deity of Jesus Christ. Roy's controversy with Marshman (of the Serampore Mission) resulted in Roy's espousal of Unitarianism and his formation in 1828 of a 'Theistic Church', which is better known as the *Brahma Samaj*.[22] Thus, as M. M. Thomas once observed, Marshman's

19 Sen Gupta, *The Christian Missionaries in Bengal*, 114.

20 Ibid., 16.

21 Ibid., 169-170.

22 Sen Gupta, *The Christian Missionaries in Bengal*, 173, 177.

impatience and zealous Christian orthodoxy cost the Indian Church the possibility of Roy as its first brilliant Bengali theologian.

## Keshub Chundra Sen

Bengal produced a number of scholars who responded creatively to the Christian challenge. Among them none was more controversial than the flamboyant Keshub Chundra Sen (1838-1884) who struggled to comprehend and express Christ in Indian terms. Unlike Ram Mohan Roy, Keshub had no difficulty with the Christian concept of Incarnation. Attracted to Jesus, Keshub never became identified with mainline institutional Christianity. Christian writers therefore have regarded him a Hindu. A leader of the *Brahmo Samaj*, he became head of a *Brahmo* faction which he named the Church of the New Dispensation and utilised to propagate Christian ideas and values. His method was borrowed from Hindu tradition. 'Keshub made it abundantly clear that he had chosen Christ as his Lord, but there is no evidence that Keshub's master was necessarily attached to the Christian religion'.[23] He used Hindu symbols, sometimes combined with Christian concepts. His concern was with 'disseminating the spirit of Christ in India'. Keshub hoped to unite East and West. He wanted India to come to Christ, 'to the feet of my sweet Jesus...'. He urged the missionaries to stop presenting Christ as an Englishman because the picture of a foreign Christianity is repugnant to Indians and 'hinders the progress of the true spirit of Christianity in this country'.

Keshub's attempt represents a spontaneous response to the gospel from within Hindu society expressed in Indian culture and symbol. At a time when Christianity was seen as part of an aggressive European civilisation, Keshub begged his contemporaries to distinguish Christianity from Western customs. To Keshub, Christ came as an Asian kinsman to fulfill the Hindu longing for union with God.

23 David C. Scott, ed., *Keshub Chunder Sen*, Madras: CLS, and Bangalore: United Theological College, 1979, 1-42.

## Brahmabandhab Upadhyaya

Another important Bengali figure was Brahmabandhab Upadhyaya (1861-1907) who went beyond Keshub by membership in the Catholic Church. A Hindu by birth, he became a Christian by spiritual rebirth, calling himself a Hindu Catholic. Hindu in custom, spiritually a Christian, Upadhyaya believed that the best in the Hindu character is made better by Christ. He distinguished *sadhana dharma* from *samaj dharma*, i.e., culture is different from faith.

In a provocative study, Staffner cites the examples of Upadhyay, Keshub and other Hindu converts to support his thesis that converts to Christ must be able to remain socially part of the Hindu community.[24] To Staffner the essence of Christianity is a faith in Jesus Christ as Saviour, received, not through rituals or ceremony, but through personal faith in Christ's promises. The entrance card to following Christ is not baptism but confession of our sinfulness and of His forgiveness. God gives Himself to us in Jesus Christ. The correction to our self-centredness is in spiritual re-birth (John 3:3) whereby we become part of a new creation (2 Corinthians 5:17). This transforming Presence is available to all through the gift of the Holy Spirit, which comes through invitation, not rituals.

Notable in the examples above is the absence of any clear expression of ecclesiology, at least not in the traditional expression of the Christian faith community. Staffner, for instance, understands Hinduism as a culture with room for many religions, Christianity as a spirituality, which can be incarnated in any culture. Staffner's study assumes the validity of a theoretical Hindu-Christian synthesis without defining the contours of the Christian faith expression within the Hindu *Samaj*. Is this sufficient?

The Church has been problematic for many Hindu converts. It was so for Bengali converts in the nineteenth century and has continued to be so as well as for others. The result has been the existence of secret followers of Christ in several localities.

24 Hans Staffner, *Jesus Christ and the Hindu Community: Is a Synthesis of Hinduism and Christianity Possible?* Anand, Gujarat: Gujarat Sahitya Prakash, 1988.

One remarkable instance, found in South India, is a group of women converts in Sivakasi, Tamil Nadu, who were not permitted to openly practice their faith. 'These Sivakasi women are Christians of a very clear character, who live daily the teaching that they have been given'.[25] Sustained by the Bible, prayer and sacraments these women have transmitted the faith over several generations despite difficulties and persecution.

## K. Subba Rao

Quite different is the response of K. Subba Rao (1912-1981). Dubbed the 'Christ-centred Healer of Andhra Pradesh',[26] Subba Rao was born a Hindu of Kamma caste in Godavari District. At any early age he became an atheist and opposed all religion, especially the *sadhus* and priests. Having lost his health through reckless living, in 1942 Subba Rao had a vision of Christ, which became the decisive event in his life. Subba Rao was healed, and eventually began a ministry of healing which attracted multitudes. According to H. L. Richard, 'Subba Rao remained a faithful devotee and servant of Christ within the Hindu community until his death'.[27] Nevertheless, despite his confession of Christ, Subba Rao rejected the Church, its sacraments, teachings and clergy.[28] His writings consisted largely of attacks on baptism, on the church and Christianity as a religion. His rejection of Christianity and the Church must be seen as part of his critique of all religions. It also appears that Subba Rao had very little knowledge of the Bible, was interested in experience rather than doctrine, and interpreted Christ in ambiguous *advaitic* categories. Despite these shortcomings,

25 Andrew Wingate, 'The Secret Christians of Sivakasi, Tamil Nadu: one pattern of Conversion in a South Indian Town'. *Religion and Society*, XXXIII, 1, March 1986, 84.

26 H. L. Richard, 'The Christ-centred Healer of Andhra Pradesh', unpublished, undated paper, ca. 1995.

27 Ibid., 3.

28 See Kaj Baago, *The Movement Around Subba Rao: A Study of the Hindu-Christian Movement around K. Subba Rao in Andhra Pradesh*, Bangalore: CISRS, 1968. Baago's study is frequently cited in Hivner's paper (above) as well as in the study of Indian Christian theology.

H. L. Richard commends Subba Rao's as a truly contextual ministry. 'That Subba Rao appeared more Hindu than Christian is a positive rather than negative point. He is in the tradition of the apostle Paul who appeared more Gentile than Jewish'.[29] Possibly so.

As reported by David Barrett, the Subba Rao movement had 300,000 followers in 1966.[30] It is my impression that the movement has dissipated since the death of the founder-guru. However H. L. Richard reports numerous devotees of Christ remaining as well as 20 groups meeting in various places including a registered society and prayer hall at Vijayawada.[31] If so, the Subba Rao movement should be seen as a distinct phenomenon on the margins of the Christian community in India. It also is not surprising if some such groups maintain a dual identity. But we are getting ahead of our story.

It was the contention of the late scholar Bishop Stephen Neill that Christianity in India must be understood as an indigenous phenomenon, an opinion endorsed by historian Robert Frykenberg[32] and supported by numerous Indian and other recent scholars.[33]

---

29 H. L. Richard, 'The Christ-centred Healer of Andhra Pradesh', unpublished, undated paper, 11.

30 David B. Barrett, ed., *World Christian Encyclopedia,* Nairobi: Oxford University Press, 1982.

31 H. L. Richard, 'The Christ-centred Healer of Andhra Pradesh', unpublished, undated paper, 3.

32 Robert Eric Frykenberg, *Christianity in India: From Beginnings to the Present,* New York: Oxford University Press, 2008, 17.

33 See the Studies in the History of Christian Missions series edited by R. E. Frykenberg and Brian Stanley and published by Eerdmans (Grand Rapids & Cambridge) and especially titles and essays of Judith Brown, John B. Carman, Duncan Forrester, Robert Frykenberg, Dennis Hudson, Daniel Jeyaraj, Geoffrey Oddie, Richard Fox Young and others supporting the 'Indianness' of Christianity in South Asia.

Chapter 6

# Bengali Builders of the Church in the Nineteenth Century

In her study of the growth of Protestant Christian communities in Bengal during the nineteenth century, Eleanor Jackson probes the background and contributions of two notable Bengali Christians, Krishna Pal (1764-1822) and Lal Behari Dey (1824-94).

## Krishna Pal

Krishna Pal is of particular interest as the first Indian convert of the Serampore Mission, baptised on 28 December, 1800 and received into membership of the Serampore Baptist Church on the first Saturday of January,1801. A poor carpenter, and in bad health, earning about four rupees per month with which he supported his wife, sister-in-law, four daughters and an adopted son, ordained in 1804 and posted to various mission stations with a salary of twelve rupees until his death.[1] His family experienced 'upward social mobility' in that his

1 Eleanor Jackson, 'From Krishna Pal to Lal Behari Dey: Indian Builders of the Church in Bengal, 1800-1894' in *Converting Colonialism: Visions and Realities in Mission History, 1706-1914* edited by Dana L. Robert, Grand Rapids and Cambridge: Eerdmans Publishing, 2008, 168-9.

third daughter married a Brahman steward, and their son Panchoo, the first Indian student admitted to Serampore College, became an outstanding Sanskrit student.[2]

## Lal Behari Dey

Lal Behari Dey was the brilliant son of a village money-lender who relocated to Calcutta for his son's education in the General Assembly's Institution. Three years later his father died, leaving the son to struggle for his education on his own. With the aid of scholarships he graduated in 1844 about a year after his conversion. Licensed to preach in 1851 and ordained in 1855, he served several pastoral charges. Altogether Lal Behari Dey was to devote 'more than forty years as missionary and minister of the Free Church of Scotland Mission'. He also taught as professor of English literature at Government Colleges in Berhampore and in Hooghly. 'His literary output in Bengali and English was prodigious'.[3] Dey's biography of his spiritual mentor, Alexander Duff, established Duff as 'one of the heroic figures in the history of missionary education in India'.[4] Dey's critique of missionary ecclesiology caused him to champion the idea of an indigenous National Church of Bengal, which though unsuccessful, led to formation of the Christo Samaj, patterned after the Brahmo Samaj, 'the purpose of which was to abolish denominational and doctrinal barriers imported by missionaries'.[5]

2 Jackson, 'From Krishna Pal to Lal Behari Dey: Indian Builders of the Church in Bengal, 1800-1894' in *Converting Colonialism: Visions and Realities in Mission History, 1706-1914* edited by Dana L. Robert, Grand Rapids and Cambridge: Eerdmans Publishing, 2008, 169.

3 Ibid.

4 Robert Eric Frykenberg, *Christianity in India: From Beginnings to the Present*, New York: Oxford University Press, 2008, 325. Duff, who regarded Sanskrit as 'inherently evil', considered the English language a *praeparatio evangelica* and hence preferable to the vernacular Bengali for educational purposes—this in contrast to the vernacular education promoted by the Serampore missionaries.

5 Frykenberg, *Christianity in India: From Beginnings to the Present*, 190.

## Krishna Mohan Banerjea

Duff's converts were never many, but Bengal was to produce several significant Christian theologians and leaders. Krishna Mohan Banerjea (1813-1885) was one such who endeavoured to place Christianity in India on a solidly Indian platform. Following his conversion in 1832, Banerjea was ordained in 1836 and served in the Anglican Church and thereafter appointed as Professor in Bishop's College where he taught for fifteen years (1852–67). Initially critical toward Hinduism, Banerjea reversed his opinion andcame to believe that the aspirations of the Vedic *rishis* could find their fulfilment in Christ. Banerjea's Vedic Theology was a brilliant attempt to build Indian Christianity on Indian religious foundations.[6] His argument that the 'Prajapati' of the Vedas could be equated with Jesus Christ, while innovative, was not entirely satisfactory and could be faulted by Hindus as well as by Christians.[7] Whatever else may be said, his was a noteworthy attempt to relate Christianity to Hinduism, and Banerjea deserves recognition for his contribution to the early development of Indian Christian theology.

## Kali Charan Chatterjee

Another Bengali Brahman convert of note was Kali Charan Chatterjee (1839-1916), converted to Christ while attending mission school and therefore disowned by his family, described as 'Christian in spirit, in manner of life, in character, in conviction'.[8] According to his biographer, there was no other leader of the Indian Church so respected and trusted by Indians and missionaries alike. Asked the reason for his conversion, Chatterjee replied that it was the attraction of the holy and blameless life of Christ and his mercy and benevolence

6 Merigala Gabriel, 'Banerjee, Krishna Mohan' in the *Oxford Encyclopaedia of South Asian Christianity*, edited by R. E. Hedlund, J. M. Athyal, J. Kalapati and Jessica Richard,New Delhi: Oxford University Press, 2011, 57-59.

7 Ibid., 58.

8 J. C. R. Ewing, *A Prince of the Church in India: Being a Record of the life of the Rev. Kali Charam Chatterjee, D.D., for Forty-eight Years a Missionary at Hoshyarpur, Punjab, India*, New York: Fleming H. Revell, 1918, 3.

to suffering humanity.[9] Following studies in Alexander Duff's Free Church College, Chatterjee was invited to serve as Headmaster of the Mission School in Jalandhar, Punjab, which he accepted. In 1865, he accepted an appointment to a school and college begun in Lahore by John Newton and C.W. Forman of the Presbyterian Mission. During this era, Chatterjee also was licensed to preach and then ordained by the Presbytery of Ludhiana. In 1968, he and his wife were appointed to missionary service in Hoshyarpur, a vast territory with a complex population of Hindus, Muslims, Sikhs, Christians, Jains, including some thousands of Chuhras and Chamars. Response was meager until the close of 1873 when a spiritual awakening began that lasted for ten years during which hundreds confessed Christ and twenty-nine Hindu and Muslim families were baptised and joined the church.[10] As an evangelist Chatterjee is said to have had special success among the Muslim landowners as well as among wandering Muslim *faqirs*.[11] Chatterjee was politically active and served on the Hoshiarpur Municipal Committee. He was the first Moderator of the Presbyterian Church in India, and a delegate to the World Missionary Conference at Edinburgh in 1910. He was outspoken in his belief that Indian Christian Church workers should be treated as equals to the alien missionaries and given full voting rights in the mission.[12] Due to his leadership and the training of Christian teachers and catechists, a community of some 3,000 baptised Christians became firmly established at Hoshiarpur. Despite his Brahmanical background, Chatterjee was able to welcome the mass conversion

9 Ewing, *A Prince of the Church in India: Being a Record of the life of the Rev. Kali Charam Chatterjee, D.D., for Forty-eight Years a Missionary at Hoshyarpur, Punjab, India*, New York: Fleming H. Revell, 1918, 34.

10 Ibid., 57.

11 Sunil M. Caleb, 'Chatterjee, Kali Charan' in the *Oxford Encyclopaedia of South Asian Christianity*, edited by R. E. Hedlund, J. M. Athyal, J. Kalapati and Jessica Richard, New Delhi: Oxford University Press, 2011, 150.

12 Caleb, 'Chatterjee, Kali Charan'.

movement among the illiterate and degraded Chuhras (sweepers, scavengers) as a genuine work of God's grace.[13]

## Kali Charan Banerjea

Kali Charan Banerjea (?1845-?1907) likewise was born into a Brahman family, then studied in Duff's college where he became a Christian and was baptised on 28 February, 1864.[14] In 1870, Banerjea together with several friends founded *The Bengal Christian Herald* (later renamed *The Indian Christian Herald*), with Joy Govinda Shome his co-editor. Several articles in this magazine called for independence of the church in Bengal from the control of the missionaries, and others argued for Hindu customs to be retained or modified for use in Christian worship. In 1877, Banerjea and J.G. Shome organised the Bengali Christian Conference, which criticised the missionaries for importing their theological and denominational differences to India. In 1887, Banerjea and Shome left their churches to form the Calcutta Christo Samaj as an expression of Christian unity, hoping thereby to eliminate all denominations. This did not prove effective, and after seven years the Christo Samaj was dissolved in 1894. When the National Missionary Society (NMS) formed in 1905, Kali Charan Banerjea was one of its founding members. He is considered a pioneer of Indigenous Christianity.[15]

## Brahmabhandav Upadhyaya

Brahmabhandav Upadhyaya (1861-1907), born Bhavani Charan Banerjea, was drawn to Christianity through his fascination with the sinless life of Jesus. Baptised on 26 February, 1891 by an Anglican priest, six months later he joined the Roman Catholic Church.

13 Ewing, *A Prince of the Church in India: Being a Record of the life of the Rev. Kali Charam Chatterjee, D.D., for Forty-eight Years a Missionary at Hoshyarpur, Punjab, India*, New York: Fleming H. Revell, 1918, 63-65.

14 Sunil M. Caleb, 'Banerjea, Kali Charan' in the *Oxford Encyclopaedia of South Asian Christianity*, edited by R. E. Hedlund, J. M. Athyal, J. Kalapati and Jessica Richard, New Delhi: Oxford University Press, 2011, 57.

15 Ibid.

In December, 1894 he donned the saffron garb of a *sannyasi* and publicly adopted the name Brahmabhandav Upadhyaya. After joining the nationalist movement in 1898, he began saying that he was 'a "Hindu" by birth but a Catholic Christian by sacramental rebirth'.[16] He was a positive rather than a confrontational approach. Prior to his conversion, Upadhyaya had been influenced by Keshab Chandra Sen (1838-1884) and the Brahmo Samaj. 'Even as a Christian, Upadhyay expected continuity with his own Hindu tradition at a time when others looked only for discontinuity'.[17] Accordingly, he is the first Indian Christian to appropriate Sankara and the Vedas for articulating Christian theology in India – for which he can be considered 'the Father of Indian Christian theology'.[18] Upadhyay understood the importance of indigenous philosophy for laying a solid foundation for Christian theology. In a recent publication, Indian theologian Samuel Rayan pays tribute to Brahmabandhay Upadhyaya for his hymn, *Vande Saccidanandam*, for its insights into the Mystery of the Trinity—insights derived from Upanisadic and Vedantic sources.[19]

Upadhyay is of current interest today because of his redefinition of Hinduism. 'Upadhyaya helped to construct an understanding of Hinduism which was no longer tied to some form of Hindu religious beliefs, but was rather the multifarious reflections of Indian culture'.

---

16 Robert Eric Frykenberg, *Christianity in India: From Beginnings to the Present*, New York: Oxford University Press, 2008, 325. Duff, who regarded Sanskrit as 'inherently evil', considered the English language a *praeparatio evangelica* and hence preferable to the vernacular Bengali for educational purposes—this in contrast to the vernacular education promoted by the Serampore missionaries. 413.

17 Timothy C. Tennent, *Building Christianity on Indian Foundations: The Legacy of Brahmabandhav Upadhyay*, Delhi: ISPCK, 2000, 9.

18 K. P. Aleaz, 'The Theological Writings of Brahmabandhav Upadhyaya Re-Examined', 77, cited by Tennent, *Building Christianity on Indian Foundations*, 7.

19 Samuel Rayan, 'A Dealer in Gems' in *Co-Worker for Your Joy: Festschrift in honour of George Gispert-Sauch S.J.*, Delhi: Vidyajyoti College & ISPCK, 2006, 20.

Rather than a particular belief system, Hinduism should be seen as a reflection of Indian culture, and it was in that sense that Upadhyaya understood himself as a Hindu Christian. Upadhyaya was committed to the truth that God has acted in history 'in a final and unique way' in Jesus Christ, that he did so contextually in a particular history and time, and that he wants to reveal Christ to India 'in Indian garb'.[20] Unfortunately the Church was not ready in Upadhyaya's day to shed its foreign image and become rooted in Indian soil.

## The *Bhakti* Movement

It is noteworthy that many converts had previously belonged to some *bhatki* group. The *bhakti* movement was prominent in Bengal with numbers of gurus and groups derived from the fifteenth-century charismatic poet Chaitanya (1486-1533) who sang of the love of God Krishna. As Jackson notes, 'Love of Krishna could more easily become love of Christ', that is to say, devotional experience rather than philosophical discourse was more effective in moving many to follow Christ. Krishna Pal, for example, prior to his conversion to Christ, had been a wandering religious mendicant.[21]

Converts in Bengal appear to have come from a variety of caste backgrounds, principally *kayast* (writer) caste followed by Brahmans and respectable Sudras, i.e., tradespeople, cultivators and artisans, but not many from the so-called untouchables and outcastes. Fear of the landowners seems to have been a major deterrent to conversion of the more vulnerable sections of society.[22] Creation of separate Christian villages was an attempted solution, not entirely successful.

Whatever their background might be, converts from the very beginning were pressed into service as catechists and preachers,

20 Tennent, *Building Christianity on Indian Foundations: The Legacy of Brahmabandhav Upadhyay*, 9,12.

21 Jackson, 'From Krishna Pal to Lal Behari Dey: Indian Builders of the Church in Bengal, 1800-1894' in *Converting Colonialism: Visions and Realities in Mission History, 1706-1914* edited by Dana L. Robert, Grand Rapids and Cambridge: Eerdmans Publishing, 2008, 174.

22 Ibid., 172.

evangelists and pastors. Sometimes converts brought special talents, which were utilised for the spiritual enrichment of the Christian community. Krishna Pal, for example, was a *bhajan* singer who continued his practice of 'singing devotional songs all night long when he became a Christian'. He also wrote a number of Bengali hymns for use in the Bengali Church.

Another gifted musician in the Serampore Mission was a village school teacher named Tarachand Datta who 'poured out books, tracts, hymns, and a Life of Christ in Bengali verse' and whose Bengali lyrics were sung for several decades.[23]

Reasons for discouragement would have been many, despite which Christianity managed to take root and grow. How so? Not to be overlooked is the individualistic 'experiential' nature of the evangelical religion brought by the pioneer missionaries and chaplains 'defined as a deep personal faith based on their continuing experience of God's mercy and forgiveness....expressed as guilt for one's sinfulness before a righteous God, acceptance of forgiveness through Jesus Christ, and the transformation of one's moral and spiritual life.[24]

Religious experience likewise is prominent in the Hindu *bhakti* movement in which the devotee expresses a feeling of unworthiness or inadequacy before the overwhelming grace of God. This could act as a bridge to faith in Christ – as seen in the poetry of Narayan Vaman Tilak and the theology of A.P. Appasamy.[25] But, that is getting ahead of our story.

---

23 Jackson, 'From Krishna Pal to Lal Behari Dey: Indian Builders of the Church in Bengal, 1800-1894' in *Converting Colonialism: Visions and Realities in Mission History, 1706-1914* edited by Dana L. Robert, Grand Rapids and Cambridge: Eerdmans Publishing, 2008, 187.

24 Ibid., 189.

25 Ibid., note 67, 189.

Chapter 7

# North India Builders of the Church in the Nineteenth Century

From Bengal with its challenges as well as brilliant contributions to the story of Christianity in India, we turn to new beginnings in other regions of Northern India, starting with Punjab.[1]

## Punjab and Ditt

Apart from earlier visitors and some Jesuits at the Mughal court in Lahore in 1595 and their converts, who migrated to Agra in 1614,[2] Christianity had no permanent presence in Punjab until the arrival of John Lowrie and the American Presbyterian missionaries at Ludhiana in 1834. Attracted by the presence of the Sikhs who were assumed to be receptive, the missionaries found better initial response to their preaching from the Chamars. But, the most significant encounter was with the rural Chuhras.

1 Information in this section is primarily from John Webster and James Massey who are the leading authorities, as well as from other available sources.

2 John C. B. Webster, 'Punjab' in the *Oxford Encyclopaedia of South Asian Christianity*, edited by R. E. Hedlund, J. M. Athyal, J. Kalapati and Jessica Richard, New Delhi: Oxford University Press, 2011, 572.

'Beginning in the 1870s and growing until the 1920s when it tapered off, there was a mass conversion movement to Christianity among the Chuhras that dramatically increased the Indian Christian population of the Punjab'.[3] The Chuhras have been described as totally dependent and powerless agricultural day labourers and scavengers.[4] As to religion they tended to adopt the religion of the dominant group in their villages be it Muslim, Sikh, Hindu. Apart from that they had their own animistic belief in evil spirits and ghosts, and relied upon *faqirs, bhagats* and *pirs* to drive them away.[5] A distinctive Chuhra feature centered in the worship of Bala Shah, 'a devotee and priest of God whom God had exalted' and in whom his followers can take refuge for protection and mercy, especially on the day of resurrection.[6] Similarities to Christian beliefs, parallels or significant contact points for the gospel can be seen in the Bala Shah tradition.

The Chuhra conversion movement began at their own initiative, started by a lame illiterate man named Ditt. Ditt was an independent Chuhra businessman engaged in buying and selling hides. Ditt heard the Christian message, not from missionaries or mission workers, but from a young Hindu Jat in a neighbouring village who had been baptised in November 1872. Ditt was convinced. In June 1873 Ditt accompanied his friend to Sialkot and was introduced to the missionary, the Rev. Samuel Martin. 'Ditt quickly convinced Martin that he already both understood the gospel well and believed it sincerely enough to receive baptism'. Following his baptism, Ditt

3 John C. B. Webster, 'Dalits and Christianity in Colonial Punjab: Cultural Interactions' in *Christians, Cultural Interactions, and India's Religious Traditions*, edited by Judith M. Brown and Robert Eric Frykenberg, Grand Rapids & Cambridge: Eerdmans Publishing, 2002, 93.

4 Ibid., 94, 101.

5 They also believed in omens, sorcery, magic, the evil eye, charms, auspicious and inauspicious times, and joined in the worship of Muslim saints, the smallpox deity, and Gugga Pir who was believed to protect people from snake bite.

6 Webster, 'Dalits and Christianity in Colonial Punjab: Cultural Interactions' in *Christians, Cultural Interactions, and India's Religious Traditions*, 95-97.

returned to his village and work. In August, he returned to Sialkot with his wife, daughter, and two neighbours whom he had convinced. The following February (1874) he brought four more neighbours to Sialkot where they also were baptised. By the time of their next annual meeting (1875) the missionaries realised that a Chuhra conversion movement was under way. This was the largest, but not the only such conversion movement among the Chuhras. Two other movements, also within the boundaries of the Sialkot mission, began near Gujranwala and Gurdaspur. 'Each spread because of the efforts of Ditt and others like him'.[7]

Along the way there was opposition despite which Ditt persisted. By 1884, eleven years after his baptism, Ditt had brought more than 500 from his caste into the Christian faith. By 1900, half the people of his community had confessed Christ, and by 1915 almost all the Chuhras of Sialkot District had become Christians.[8]

'The main cause for the mass movement to Christianity was that it attempted to humanise those who have been dehumanised'.[9] By 1884 and 1885, the Chuhra movement had spread beyond the Sialkot mission, and neighbouring missions had become involved as well. Wherever there was a significant number of inquirers or converts, it was the practice of the missions to send a catechist or teacher to that village to instruct them. Generally this person was a Chuhra who had been trained for his tasks, which included home visitation, instruction in basic Christian beliefs, conducting daily prayers, and Sunday worship, and instructions for establishing a

7 Webster, 'Dalits and Christianity in Colonial Punjab: Cultural Interactions' in *Christians, Cultural Interactions, and India's Religious Traditions*, 99.

8 James Massey, 'Holy Spirit Led Mission in North India' in *Missiology for the 21st Century: South Asian Perspectives*, edited by Roger E. Hedlund and Paul Joshua Bhakiaraj, Delhi: ISPCK, Chennai: MIIS, 2004, 255.

9 Michael Anikuzhikattil, 'Punjab: Catholic Mission In' in the *Oxford Encyclopaedia of South Asian Christianity*, edited by R. E. Hedlund, J.M. Athyal, J. Kalapati and Jessica Richard,New Delhi: Oxford University Press, 2011, 572.

Sunday School.[10] James Massey makes the point that 'The gospel in reality was incarnated into the Punjabi culture through the writings of Punjabi Christians'.[11]

It is estimated that 90 percent of the Church today in northwest India and in Pakistan are descendants from this people movement. Despite their lack of education, the Chuhra converts themselves proved to be the most effective rural evangelists among their own people. After 1881, the Presbyterian Mission opened many village schools for Christian children and Sunday Schools for both children and adults. The number of Chuhra Christian communicants in the Presbyterian Church rose dramatically to around 45,000 by 1930.[12]

## Tribal India

India is a land inhabited by numerous minorities, among them several hundred different tribes, each with its own language and culture. The backbone of Tribal India is a wide strip of land stretching from Mumbai to Kolkata consisting of mountains, hills and valleys. The tribal inhabitants have suffered exploitation, oppression and abuse.

10 Webster, 'Dalits and Christianity in Colonial Punjab: Cultural Interactions' in *Christians, Cultural Interactions, and India's Religious Traditions*, 100,102.

11 Important names include Padri Daud Singh, a Sikh convert and possibly the first Punjabi Christian poet; Tahil Singh who gave us 'The Story of Jesus Christ in Punjabi Verse' in 126 pages, published by the Punjab Religious Book Society, Anarkali, Lahore in 1900; Padri Iman-ul-Din Shahbaz, a poet and great scholar who rendered the entire Book of Psalms in metrical Punjabi verse and adapted to local Punjabi tunes, his Punjabi Zabur a contribution to the entire Indian Church; Musa Khan whose narrative poem based on the Biblical story of Esther was to encourage readers to live and die for others; Jwahar Das whose story of Joseph in Punjabi verse is well-known among the common people. [James Massey, 'Punjabi Christian Writers' Response to the Gospel' in the *Oxford Encyclopaedia of South Asian Christianity*, edited by R. E. Hedlund, J. M. Athyal, J. Kalapati and Jessica Richard,New Delhi: Oxford University Press, 2011, 573.]

12 Freda Margaret Carey, 'Ditt and the Chuhra Mass Movement' in the *Oxford Encyclopaedia of South Asian Christianity*, edited by R. E. Hedlund, J. M. Athyal, J. Kalapati and Jessica Richard,New Delhi: Oxford University Press, 2011, 229.

Deprived of economic and political power to decide their destiny—their culture denigrated, mother tongue ignored and educational access limited --'the Tribals are caught up in a deep and horrendous crisis for survival'.[13] This is the background against which Christian missionaries in the mid-nineteenth century came with the love of God for all people including the tribals.

The Chotanagpur region (comprising Jharkhand and parts of Chhattisgarh, Orissa and West Bengal) is inhabited by a large number of *adivasis* [original inhabitants]. Throughout the nineteenth century (more precisely from 1771 to 1900) a series of revolts against British rule took place as the *adivasis* tried to protect and reclaim their ancestral land from the clutches of unscrupulous landlords. The succession of rebellions involved the Santhals, Bhumij, Chero, Oraons, Munda, Ho and Kol tribes. The British using armed force quelled each uprising. To the disheartened Tribal people the loss of the land meant not only a loss of identity, but also the failure of religion. No longer did the tribal gods come to their aid. Was religion powerless? It was at this time of disillusionment and bewilderment that the missionaries came, first the Lutherans, then the Catholics. The tribals felt that 'God had heard their cry and had sent them a friend to stand by them and treat them with love and sympathy'.[14] Pietist Protestant missionaries from Germany, as well as Jesuits from Belgium, stood with the tribal people in their struggle against oppressive treatment by the Zamindars, and the Chotanagpur tribals in large numbers were attracted to Christianity.[15] Fr Constant Lievens in particular is remembered with great appreciation for his legal interventions through the Civil Court.[16] Lievens made himself

13 Mathew George Kariapuram, 'Education for Change: Justice to the Tribals' in *Transforming Religion: Prospects for a New Society* edited by Felix Wilfred, Delhi: ISPCK, 2009, 161.

14 Nirmal Minz, 'Missiology for Twenty First Century Tribal India' in *Missiology for the 21st Century: South Asian Perspectives*, edited by Roger E. Hedlund and Paul Joshua Bhakiaraj, Delhi: ISPCK, Chennai: MIIS, 2004, 405.

15 Ibid., 406.

16 Linus Kujur, 'Lievens, Constant' in the *Oxford Encyclopaedia of South Asian Christianity*, edited by R. E. Hedlund, J. M. Athyal, J. Kalapati and Jessica

the champion of the oppressed, providing lawyers to help fight cases in courts of law. Thousands left the Lutherans to join the Catholic Church, thousands of pagans followed, and in 1891 when he returned to Belgium the exhausted Lievens left behind a Church of 79,000 baptised Christians.[17] Still today, Jharkhand remains a centre of Roman Catholic vitality in North India.

But there is more. Not too far away the Santal Mission of the Northern Churches, begun by a duo of Scandinavian Pietists, Lars Olsen Skrefsrud (1840-1910) from Norway and H.P. Börresen (1825-1901) from Denmark, were engaged with the Santal Adivasis. In 1868 the Indian Home Mission to the Santals was founded. After a slow start, the mission progressed with several hundred village leaders requesting baptism. The Mission also engaged in social work and famine relief work, and in this way established itself as 'a buffer between the Santals and Hindu moneylenders'.[18] Skrefsrud proved a gifted linguist who composed a grammar of the Santali language, a classic said to be still in use. He also sought to Christianise the people, but without unnecessarily disrupting their manner of life. By the time of Skrefsrud's death in 1910 Santali adherents were reported to number 15,000.[19] Growing from this beginning, the Northern Evangelical Lutheran Church (NELC) is a constituent member of the United Evangelical Lutheran Churches in India and also participates in other evangelical and ecumenical organisations and projects.

Education is known to be 'the key catalyst to the development of human resources'. Tribal education is vital to combat the debilitating poverty, illiteracy, underdevelopment, exploitation and land

---

Richard, New Delhi: Oxford University Press, 2011, 398.

17 Stephen Neill, *A History of Christian Missions*, Baltimore: Penguin Books, 1964, 405.

18 Peter B. Andersen, 'Revival from a Native Point of View: Proselytization of the Indian Home Mission and the Kherwar Movement among the Santals' in *Christians, Cultural Interactions, and India's Religious Traditions* edited by Judith M. Brown and Robert Eric Frykenberg, Grand Rapids & Cambridge: Eerdmans Publishing, and London: RoutledgeCurzon, 2002, 123.

19 Ibid., 362.

alienation, which are characteristic of tribal India.[20] How tragic that the Constitution of India 'does not recognise even one of the eighty-odd languages of the adivasis'.[21]

As Minz points out, it was the missionaries who brought education, health and economic development to the tribals. The missionaries put tribal languages into written form, compiled grammars, and translated the Bible into tribal languages. Today's Tribal Christians and Tribal Churches possess the spiritual heritage and capability to respond creatively to the current crisis of identity, which is at the heart of the struggle to survive. Social as well as spiritual transformation is taking place. 'Our non-Christian neighbours notice the transformation of tribal life' as inner change is reflected in a life-style of healthy and clean practices adopted by tribal Christians.

Today 'Tribal Christians form about 24.5 percent of the total Christian population of India'. The dynamic Indian missionary movement also is focused on Tribal India, and a majority of Indian missionaries serve among Tribals.Today thousands of new believers are baptised and handed over to the nearest denominational church, and in this way the redemptive activity of the Church will continue and spread.[22]

Nirmal Minz, himself a Chotanagpur tribal Christian leader and ecclesiastical figure (bishop), social activist and well-known scholar, clearly states that the Tribal Christians are the most effective witnesses to their own people, but that programmes of social action and wholistic service to the larger community require outside help including both personnel and finance. A call therefore is issued for partnership between Tribal Churches and cooperating outside agencies.[23]

---

20 Kariapuram, 'Education for Change: Justice to the Tribals' in *Transforming Religion: Prospects for a New Society,* 162, 167, 172, 174.

21 G. N. Devy, *A Nomad Called Thief: Reflections on Adivasi Silence*, Hyderabad: Orient Longmans, 2006, 13.

22 Minz, 'Missiology for Twenty First Century Tribal India' in *Missiology for the 21st Century: South Asian Perspectives*, 399, 406-412.

23 Ibid., 411.

Chapter 8

# Social/Religious Change in the Nineteenth Century India

Mission among *adivasis* (Tribals) was but one sector of Christian outreach during the nineteenth century. Another consisted of efforts among oppressed peoples known today as Dalits (formerly Untouchables or Outcastes). An interesting case is found in Chhattisgarh among former Chamars who had become followers of Guru Ghasidas and were now known as 'Satnamis'.

## *Chhattisgarhisation* of Christianity

Guru Ghasidas was a Chamar who, following family tragedy, emerged from a six-month forest retreat to become a reformer. His followers were to abandon idol worship and should devote themselves only to *Satnam*(True Name)—the one and only formless deity from which Ghasidas had received a message for the Chamars. They were to avoid eating meat, should renounce the use of tobacco and alcohol, and must keep away from defiling occupations.[1] These lifestyle changes

1 Chad M. Bauman, *Christian Identity and Dalit Religion in Hindu India, 1868-1947*, Grand Rapids & Cambridge: Eerdmans Publishing, 2008, 44.

were clearly borrowed from Hindu notions of purity and pollution by which the Guru hoped to enhance the status of his followers. Indian sociologists describe this dynamic as *Sanskritisation*,[2] a process by which lower status groups imitate the vegetarianism and other practices of so-called higher castes by which the lower status group lays claim to an imagined earlier higher caste status hoping thereby to enhance their position in a hierarchical society.

But, there was more: a prophecy of the arrival of a 'white-faced man with a book under his arm'. Into this context in 1868, eighteen years after the death of Ghasidas, came the first Christian missionary, the Rev. Oscar Lohr, having heard about this prophecy, to preach the gospel to the Satnamis. At Raipur, Lohr opened a school for Satnamis, thinking thus to prepare leaders for the future church. In his preaching Lohr identified the 'True Name' with the name of Jesus Christ.[3] Lohr seems to have understood himself to be the 'white-faced man' of the prophecy, and therefore that the Satnamis were ready to accept the gospel.[4] Events following, however, suggest a more complex scenario.

At first growth was slow, Satnamis joining the Evangelical Church in small groups, then in times of famine as the mission fed thousands, 'Chhattisgarhis became Christian in droves', although many later reverted to their previous faiths.[5] Nevertheless a small percentage of Satnamis did become and remain Christians. Their conversion did not lead to the Christianisation of Chhattisgarh. Rather, as Bauman finds in his study, more than the numbers might suggest, what really

2 The term *Sanskritisation* was coined by the late well-known Indian sociologist, M. N. Srinivas, *Social Change in Modern India*, Berkeley: University of California Press, 1966; New Delhi: Orient Longman, 1995 reprint; also see his *Caste in Modern India: and Other Essays,* Bombay: Media Promoters & Publishers, 1962.

3 Bauman, *Christian Identity and Dalit Religion in Hindu India, 1868-1947*, Grand Rapids & Cambridge: Eerdmans Publishing, 2008, 60.

4 Ibid., 106-8. Bauman points out that there were several versions of the prophecy as well as some doubts as to its authenticity.

5 Bauman, *Christian Identity and Dalit Religion in Hindu India, 1868-1947*, Grand Rapids & Cambridge: Eerdmans Publishing, 2008, 64-65.

has taken place is the *Chhattisgarhisation* of Christianity in which pre-existing Chhattisgarhi values, hopes and dreams find fulfillment in Christian *dharma*.[6] That this might also have included appropriation and reconfiguration of upper-caste Hindu traditions and behaviour would serve the Satnami quest for improved social status for which Christianity proved an effective vehicle.[7] 'The community did not simply accept Christianity as it was presented to them, but rather, consciously or unconsciously, extracted from the encounter with western Christians those things that best helped them respond to the physical, spiritual, and social exigencies of their time and place'.[8]

The early missionaries stressed the continuity between Christianity and the message of Guru Ghasidas, of Christianity as the fulfillment of the latter.[9] Christianity provided an escape from inconvenient or expensive rituals, and at the same time the Satnami Christians absorbed new values.[10] Indian evangelists as well as the missionaries portrayed conversion as the next logical step for the followers of Ghasidas. Statistical reports indicate the total number of Satnami converts since 1868 as three to four thousand in all of Chhattisgarh, and that by the late 1930s they comprised a community of 15,000 Satnami Christians including children and grandchildren.[11]

## Hill Tribes of Assam

Another Christian centre was beginning to develop in the Northeastern part of India in the region of Assam. In the year 1813, Pastor Krishna Pal had been sent by the Serampore Baptist

6 Bauman, *Christian Identity and Dalit Religion in Hindu India, 1868-1947*, Grand Rapids & Cambridge: Eerdmans Publishing, 2008, 6.

7 Ibid., 188. See also Donald A. McGavran, *The Satnami Story: a thrilling drama of religious change*, Pasadena, CA: Wm. Carey Library, 1990.

8 Bauman, *Christian Identity and Dalit Religion in Hindu India, 1868-1947*, Grand Rapids & Cambridge: Eerdmans Publishing, 2008, 228.

9 Ibid., 104.

10 Ibid., 80-81.

11 Ibid., 66, 107.

Mission to work among the Khasi people of the present state of Meghalaya.[12] Despite its apparent success, the Khasi mission had to be discontinued and Krishna Pal recalled as the Serampore Mission was unable to provide continued support following the demise of Joshua Marshman at Serampore in 1837. Meanwhile in 1836, the American Baptist Mission had arrived in upper Assam and begun work which soon spread to Nagaland, Manipur, Garo Hills, Arunachal and other parts of the region. Later the British Baptist Mission entered Mizoram (then known as the Lushai Hills) and experienced rapid growth among the Mizos as well as some neighbouring tribes. In 1841, the Welsh Calvinistic Methodists arrived to work among the Khasis and soon also had significant impact also in Mizoram, Manipur, and among the Cachar and other tribes in Assam. The Catholic Mission came later in 1890 but would soon make significant contributions to the region.

The Protestant missionaries were products of Pietism, of revivals and the Evangelical awakening in Europe and America who came to India to preach the Good News of God's salvation for all people. Neither sponsored nor supported by the colonial powers, they brought their own resources for implementing their vision. This involved starting schools and colleges, providing alphabets and reducing languages to writing, production of books. 'Evangelization had tremendous social consequences and contributed to national integration'. Literature and literacy had a unifying impact on the tribes.

The hill tribes of the Northeast did not have a common intelligible language. The selection of a particular dialect for translation purposes contributed to the development of a solidified community which had tremendous implications for social transformation. Gradually, the missionaries produced books, booklets, hymnals, Bible translations and other literature in the languages of the people. These publications

12 O. L. Snaitang, 'Christianity as Social Transformation in North East India' in *Missiology for the 21st Century: South Asian Perspectives*, edited by Roger E. Hedlund and Paul Joshua Bhakiaraj, Delhi: ISPCK, Chennai: MIIS, 2004, 387. Information in this section on North East India is drawn primarily from this source, 387-392.

laid the foundation for creating indigenous literature which contributed to a sense of common identity. Literature 'solidified the once fragmented tribe'. Schools were opened in order to teach reading and writing, without which it was believed the preaching of the gospel would not have lasting results. 'Christianity and education went side by side in the region'. Educational institutions and medical services provided by the missions also were effective for counteracting superstitions and for worldview change. The Christian missions, states history scholar Snaitang, brought an alternative faith which created 'a solidified society and an inclusive culture'.[13]

Consider Nagaland: when the first American Baptist missionaries, Edward W. Clark and his wife Mary, arrived in 1872, 'it was considered extremely risky to minister the Nagas' headhunting culture. But, the Clarks served faithfully for 21 years in the hill country and helped establish a lasting Christian influence. By the 1890s, the British, who maintained a colonial presence in Nagaland, had outlawed headhunting'.[14] Today Nagaland is known as 'the most Baptist state in the world' (60 percent of Nagaland's population of 1.9 million are Baptists) and vying to become 'a powerhouse for cross-cultural missions'.[15] Not only Nagaland, but also in Mizoram, Manipur and Meghalaya, Protestant Churches under local leaders are engaged in mission among other ethnic groups both in India and beyond.[16]

## Anglican Reassesments in South India

South India remained a major centre of Christian influence and growth during the nineteenth century. For the Anglican Church in India it was a time for introspection. It was the height of the colonial era in which 'the Indian Ecclesiastical Establishment (IEE) involved

13 Snaitang, 'Christianity as Social Transformation in North East India' in *Missiology for the 21st Century: South Asian Perspectives*, 388-390.

14 Manpreet Singh, 'The Soul Hunters of Central Asia' available at http://www.christianitytoday.com/ct/2006/002/38.51.html, accessed on 18/11/11.

15 Ibid.

16 Snaitang, 'Christianity as Social Transformation in North East India' in *Missiology for the 21st Century: South Asian Perspectives*, 391.

government in the enrollment of clergy, their distribution, and their ministrations'.[17] Not surprisingly there were critics and opposition to this arrangement. At least one official described the Anglican Church's dependence on government as 'prejudicial to the interests and advancement of religion' due to preoccupation with budgets and grants, rules and regulations[18] rather than concern for spirituality and the well-being of the population.

It also was the era which saw the beginnings of Indian nationalism. 'The nationalist movement was a development of Indian politics under an alien state'.[19] The 'Quit India' movement had particular implications for the (Established) Anglican Church in India. Among other issues there was the call for Church union in South India, and the beginnings of the Church reunion movement.[20] Meanwhile in 1885, the same year the Indian National Congress was founded, Pullney Andy had founded the National Church of India 'with a nonsectarian and inclusivist invitation'.[21] Despite its self-support and self-government, indigenous forms and symbols, this 'united' church attempt failed.

Such was also the fate of an earlier attempt in 1857 by one A. Sattampillai who broke away from the Anglican Church in Tirunelvelli to create the Hindu Christian Church (also known as *Nattar Sabai* meaning 'National Church') of which a remnant still exists as the Indian Church of the Only Saviour.[22]

---

17 Gerald Studdert-Kennedy, 'Theology and Authority, Constitution and Improvisation: The Colonial Church in India' in *Christians, Cultural Interactions, and India's Religious Traditions* edited by Judith M. Brown and Robert Eric Frykenberg, Grand Rapids & Cambridge: Eerdmans Publishing, and London: Routledge Curzon, 2002, 155.

18 Studdert-Kennedy, 'Theology and Authority, Constitution and Improvisation: The Colonial Church in India' in *Christians, Cultural Interactions, and India's Religious Traditions* .

19 Ibid., 160.

20 Ibid., 169.

21 Ibid., 170.

22 M. Thomas Thangaraj, 'The History and Teachings of the Hindu Christian Community Commonly Called Nattu Sabai in Tirunelveli', *Indian Church*

Among the significant Anglican missionary figures of the nineteenth century, Bishop Robert Caldwell deserves special mention. Under his leadership Tirunelveli became the most successful region for Christian expansion in nineteenth century India.[23] 'Acutely aware of the impermanence of missionary control of the Tirunelveli church', Caldwell systematically developed the selfhood of the church. The principles of self-support, self-propagation and self-governance were instilled along with 'the hope and promise that the future governance of the Church belonged to them and to them alone'.[24]

Caldwell was a scholar who also devoted time to 'the principal revision of the Tamil translation of the Bible, which was commenced in April 1858 and was completed in April 1869'.[25] Caldwell was aware of the shortcomings of the existing Bible translations which made revision necessary and important. He also helped revise the Tamil hymnal and 'rearranged it for use in the Anglican service'.[26]

Bishop Caldwell's pastoral motivation is seen in these projects as well as in the system of Christian teaching and discipline he developed for the spiritual well-being and growth of village Christians. The Christians in every village were to assemble twice daily for public prayer and catechization. Besides Sunday services there were to be two full services weekly 'when the entire service for the day is read, and a sermon preached'.[27] Weekly Bible classes as well as Sunday School for adults were conducted to inculcate the tenets and principles of Christianity. For those unable to read special classes were arranged in

---

*History Review*, June 1971, 43-68.

23 Y. Vincent Kumaradoss, *Robert Caldwell: A Scholar-Missionary in Colonial South India*, Delhi: ISPCK, 2008, 277.

24 Ibid., 278.

25 Ibid., 174.

26 Ibid., 177.

27 Robert Caldwell, *Lectures on the Tinnevelly Missions, Descriptive of the Field, the Work, and the Results: With Introductory Lecture on the Progress of Christianity in India*, London: Bell & Daldy, 1857, 60-64. Cited in Kumaradoss, *Robert Caldwell: A Scholar-Missionary*, 69.

which the Creed, the Lord's Prayer, the Ten Commandments, other Bible texts and parts of the Catechism were memorized.[28]

An event of importance for the Christian community but also for the emergence of modern India was the founding in 1837 of John Anderson's Institution, renamed as Madras Christian College (MCC) in 1857. MCC was one among several elite colleges in various regions of India many of them created by the Church of Scotland Mission. Among them Duff's Scottish Church College in Calcutta (1830), Wilson College in Bombay (1835), Forman Christian College in Lahore (1864), St. Stephen's College at Delhi (1870), Nobel College in Machlipatnam (1842), Hislop College in Nagpur (1844), St. John's College in Agra (1850), Guntur Christian College (1893), Isabella Thoburn College for Women at Lucknow (1886) as well as others later. Inevitably there were changes, and gradually the colleges catered to an elitist clientele the majority being non-Christians. Sophisticated missionaries including MCC Principal William Miller (1838-1923) advocated a fulfillment theory of mission according to which the object was not to convert but 'to permeate Indian society with Christian values'.[29] To do so, Miller set high standards for the College. A distinguished faculty was recruited. Miller aimed to educate the elite 'irrespective of whether they became converts or not, it was enough if they were suffused with Christian values'.[30] Through the years MCC has held to these ideals, and today MCC counts among its graduates numbers of illustrious scholars in various fields as well as political figures and national leaders. Illustrious MCC Christian graduates of the nineteenth century included A. J. Appasamy, V. S. Azariah, K.T. Paul, P. Chenchiah, V. Chakkarai, D. G. Moses, Rajaiah D. Paul and many others.

---

28 Kumaradoss, *Robert Caldwell: A Scholar-Missionary in Colonial South India*, 69.

29 Frykenberg, *Christianity in India*, 339.

30 Joshua Kalapati and Ambrose Jeyasekaran T., *Life and Legacy of Madras Christian College 1837-1978*, Chennai: Zha Communications, 2010, 117.

## Independent Churches in Kerala

During the nineteenth century Kerala experienced a number of new independent Christian movements. A Brahman convert named Yusthus Joseph became a popular revivalist preacher, and was ordained by the CMS (Church Missionary Society) Anglicans in 1869. Rev. Yusthus Joseph brought the revival movement into both the Anglican (CMS Church) and the Mar Thoma Church. Joseph was a great hymn writer whose hymns continue to be sung at the famous Maramon Convention and in the Kerala churches. However Joseph was suspected of heresy because he expected the Second Coming of Christ to take place in 1881. Therefore in 1875, the [Anglican] CMS Church excommunicated Joseph, and in that same year he founded the Kannetti Revival Church. When Jesus did not return to earth as predicted, most of the people left the new church. Despite their disillusionment with his teachings and prophesies, Yusthus Joseph is considered a Christian by the Christians of Kerala who continue to use his hymns in worship. Out of 427 hymns in a hymnal of the Mar Thoma Church, 26 are by Yusthus Joseph. In 1887, at the age of 52 Yusthus Joseph passed away and is buried at the CSI (Anglican) church in Kannetti.[31] This movement was said to be the product of ferment created by the translation and publication of the Bible in Malayalam. Kerala has had a number of such Independent Christian movements.

Whether conversion movements among Dalits in Chhatisgarh or hill tribes in Assam, Mizoram or Nagaland as well as revival movements in Tirunelveli or Kerala, such movements were inspired and guided by significant spiritual leaders.

31 'Vidhuwan Kutty Achen (Rev. Yusthus Joseph) 1835-1887: Life story of a Priest who wrote 26 Hymns in the Kristheeya Keerththanangal (Hymn Book of the Mar Thoma Church)', Published by Thomas John Philip Nalloor, Nalloor Publications, Kuriannoor 689550, Kerala, India. Available online at Vidhuwant Kutty Achen.pdf , accessed on 18/11/11.

Chapter 9

# Reformers and Reforms in the Nineteenth Century India

Movements social and religious have been many, some less effective, others successful, each manifesting the charisma of particular leaders.

## Jyotirao Phule

Western India and more specifically Maharashtra 'is a land of social thinkers, social reformers and social revolutionaries'[1] that has produced a number of important reformers not least of whom is Jyotirao Phule (1827-1890) of Pune. Mahatma[2] Phule—for so he became known—is of special interest for several reasons. Pune was a

1 Dilip Walse-Patil, Minister for Higher & Technical Education of the Government of Maharashtra, in his Foreword to the *Collected Works of Mahatma Jotirao Phule, Vol. 3: Cultivator's Whipcord*, Mumbai: Mahatma Jotirao Phule Source Material Publication Committee, Govt. of Maharashtra, 2002, 7.

2 The title 'Mahatma' (Great One) was spontaneously conferred upon him in 1818 by the people at a gathering in Bombay in which Jotirao Phule was felicitated. See the 'Life and Work of Mahatma Phule' by Hari Narke (ed.), the *Collected Works of Mahatma Jotirao Phule, Vol. 3: Cultivator's Whipcord*,

centre of Brahmin influence, and most social and religious reformers were Brahmins. Phule however was neither Brahmin nor from a high or middle caste, but a *Shudra* (lower caste) of the *Mali* (gardener) caste. 'Phule not only overcame the Brahmin dominance of Pune but also initiated a reform movement among the depressed classes and pioneered an anti-Brahmin movement in Maharashtra'.[3] Phule was a product of the Scottish Mission School in Pune, and he opted to teach in the girls' orphanage school of the Scottish Mission.

Perhaps his interaction with the missionaries inspired his vision of providing education for women and children of the lower castes. He began a school for girls, the 'Low-Caste Female School' in Pune. 'This he did at a time when educating the lower castes, let alone educating the female, was severely prohibited by Hindu society'.[4] His concern for widows, the poor and the lower castes appears to have been inspired by the work of the Christian missionaries. Historian M. D. David states that 'Jyotirao Phooley, the Indian pioneer in the education of women in Maharashtra, drew his inspiration from the work of the American Maratha Mission in Ahmednagar'.[5] Phule's reform took tangible form in the afore-mentioned girls' school, a series of schools for untouchables and a Home for the Prevention of Infanticide.

The liberation and education of women was central to his plan for rebuilding Hindu society. Therefore, he favoured widow remarriage but opposed polygamy and child marriage.[6] Phule's reform movement

---

Mumbai: Mahatma Jotirao Phule Source Material Publication Committee, Govt. of Maharashtra, 2002, 21.

3 Atul Y. Aghamkar and Vishwas Padole, *Christian Missions in Maharashtra: Retrospect and Prospect*, Bangalore: TETRAWPOI, 2010, 232.

4 Ibid., 232.

5 M. D. David, 'Glimpses of Socio-Religious Life in Western India During the Nineteenth Century from Church Records', *Indian Church History Review* 14/1 (June 1980), 47-48; cited by Aghamkar and Padole, *Christian Missions in Maharashtra*, 232-3.

6 Charles Heimsath, *Indian Nationalism and Hindu Social Reforms*, Princeton University Press, 1964, 238; cited by Aghamkar and Padole, *Christian Missions in Maharashtra*, 233.

included a number of Christian themes and practices. Yet so far as we know, Phule himself never became a Christian. Phule speaks of the fatherhood of God and brotherhood of man, ideas imbibed in the Christian mission school, no doubt, and denounced the Hindu caste system.[7] He said, 'God is one and all human beings are his children: that is why they are my brothers and sisters. I will treat them as brothers and sisters. I will respect women. I will give attention to educate my children in truth'.[8] In several ways, Phule gave expression to his convictions. 'He was the first caste Hindu in Poona who threw open his own well to people of all castes and creeds'.[9] To understand the plight of the farmers, he travelled on foot through many villages and visited the people hut to hut. He gave the farmers ideas for improving agriculture--and also publicized their exploitation by police, revenue officials, money lenders and landlords.

To further propagate his ideas he founded the *Satya Shodhak Samaj* (Society of Truthseekers) to which he devoted nearly seventeen years of his life. His was an anti-caste movement founded on the premise that there is only one God 'who fills the whole universe' and that 'all human beings are God's children' and each has the right to be a devotee of God without any human intermediary—and God did not create the caste system.[10] According to Phule, 'The one and only religion of the Creator is the Truth', and 'There is no other religion except the *Truth* in this world' and therefore 'The true humanitarian religion consists in truthful conduct'.[11] While not a Christian, Phule

7 Aghamkar and Padole, *Christian Missions in Maharashtra: Retrospect and Prospect*, 234.

8 Sunil Sardar and Thom Wolf, *Phule in His Own Words*, New Delhi: University Institute, n.d., 73.

9 Hari Narke (ed.), 'Life and Work of Mahatma Phule' in *Collected Works of Mahatma Jotirao Phule, Vol. 3: Cultivator's Whipcord*, 20.

10 Ibid., 21-22.

11 Jotirao Phule, *Collected Works of Mahatma Jotirao Phule, Vol. II, Selections*, Bombay: Education Department, Government of Maharashtra, 1991, 85, 86.

noted approvingly that many of the farmers of his day had 'embraced the Christian faith and achieved a human status'.[12]

Phule speaks of the tradition of King Bala, 'the original King of this land' as 'an embodiment of all virtues' which his subjects remember gratefully 'on the occasion of Dassera and Diwali' at which the Kshatriya women fervently pray, 'Let all evil flee far from hence, and let Bali's Kingdom come!'[13] But Phule went further in that he related this ancient prophecy to the coming of Jesus Christ:

> The universal Creator of us all and our universal Father the Almighty God—so ordained that the sacred knowledge of the Truth and human rights that he generously bestowed on us all should be enjoyed by us all in amity and harmony. To translate this desire of the Almighty into reality, ***Baliraja, the champion of the oppressed,***the holy, the repository of the wisdom, and who always spoke the truth—manifested himself on this earth after a few years, he undertook the great mission of emancipating his depressed, oppressed and weak brethren from the trammels of the treacherous, wicked and cunning ensnarers...and strove toestablish the 'Kingdom of God' in this land of ours. *Thus the prophecy of our venerable old ladies* ***'May Bali's Kingdom Come'!*** *seems to have materialised (partially). When that* ***Baliraj (Jesus Christ) was crucified*** *by a few wicked desparadoes a great movement of liberation was set in motion* in Europe,and crores of people became his followers (embraced his teachings) and they strove ceaselessly to establish His kingdom on earth in consonance with the dictates of our Creator.[14]

---

12 Jotirao Phule, the *Collected Works of Mahatma Jotirao Phule, Vol. III: Cultivator's Whipcord*, edited by Hari Narke, Mumbai: Mahatma Jotirao Phule Source Material Publication Committee, Govt. of Maharashtra, 2002, 49.

13 Jotirao Phule, *Collected Works of Mahatma Jotirao Phule, Vol. II, Selections*, 152.

14 Jotirao Phule, *Collected Works of Mahatma Jotirao Phule, Vol. I, Slavery*, Bombay: Education Department, Government of Maharashtra, 1991, 36 [*emphasis* mine].

Thus, we see Mahatma Jyotirao Phule, Christian or not, whose formation is intimately linked to the person and teachings of Jesus Christ. Phule's Baliraja Proposal was a call for India to switch tracks, because in Phule's thinking, India needed a new cultural mentor and he 'recommended India to quit Manu and follow after Baliraja'.[15] The radical nature of Phule's Baliraja proposal suggests Phule not so much a reformer as a revolutionary, i.e., to be honoured as the Father of Social Revolution in India. Both Ambedkar and Gandhi acknowledged Phule as their guru.[16]

Not to be forgotten is Mahatma Phule's wife Savitribai, 'Modern India's first woman teacher, a radical exponent of mass and female education, a champion of women's liberation' who despite her importance has been bypassed in the history of modern India.[17] Social activist Gail Omvedt states that Jyotirao had taken the radical step of educating his wife so that she could educate others—over the strenuous objections of both their families—and that she became his constant companion throughout their life of struggle together.[18] 'She took part boldly in all the social revolutionary activities' of her husband, continuing his work after his death, until she died in 1897 doing social service among the victims of a plague epidemic.[19] Savitribai is important in her own right as a leader who 'encouraged a reversal of traditional subservient roles of women and depressed castes' and whose own home became a sanctuary for deserted women and orphans. She stood at 'the forefront of a socio-cultural struggle

15 Thom Wolf, *India Progress Prone: The Baliraja Proposal of Mahatma Phule*, New Delhi: University Institute, 2008, 47-48.

16 Ibid., 27-28.

17 Braj Ranjan Mani, 'Introduction' in *A Forgotten Liberator: The Life and Struggle of Savitribai Phule* edited by Braj Ranjan Mani and Pamela Sardar, New Delhi: Mountain Peak, 2008, 7.

18 Gail Omvedt, 'A Teacher and a Leader' in *A Forgotten Liberator*, edited by Braj Ranjan Mani and Pamela Sardar, 28-29.

19 Ibid., 31.

that challenged the tendency to focus only on higher social groups'.[20] Let Savitribai not be forgotten.

## Nilakantha (Nehemia) Goreh

Illustrious converts to Christianity are to be found in various locations of the Maratha country. One such was Nilakantha (Nehemia) Goreh (1825-1885) from a prominent Chitpawan Brahmin family of Bundelkhand in Central India. Goreh was a contributor of vitriolic anti-Christian, anti-missionary rhetoric against the presence of foreign missionaries in India. But four years later Goreh was a baptized Christian, not without some doubts, but repentant of his depravity, and now a devout Anglo-Catholic.[21]

How did it come about? Richard Fox Young notes that Nilakanth Goreh's conversion was not sudden but a gradual transition from a tightly circumscribed background dominated by an overprotective father and a tyrannical orthodox uncle.[22] The key to Nilakanth's radical change appears to have been the aggressive bazaar preaching of CMS missionary William Smith (1906-75) whose attack on Hinduism greatly offended young Nilakanth. Richard Young suggests that Nilakanth was in actuality a seeker to whom Smith's assault communicated *choice*, the possibility of an alternate reality. Smith's critique 'placed the Christian *dharma* in tension with the Hindu *dharma*' which provided Nilakanth the opportunity to choose his own identity. Richard Young makes the further observation that 'the early post-conversion Nilakanth was virtually the mirror image of missionary Smith': out on the streets of Benares (Varanasi) 'proclaiming the no-other-way-than-faith-in-Christ-the-*avatar*-of-God message that had irked him so much initially'.

20 Braj Ranjan Mani, 'Introduction' in *A Forgotten Liberator*, 9.

21 Samuel H. Moffett, *A History of Christianity in Asia*, Vol.I, Maryknoll: Orbis Books, 1998, 442-443.

22 Richard Fox Young, 'Enabling Encounters: The Case of Nilakanth-Nehemiah Goreh, Brahmin Convert', *International Bulletin of Missionary Research*, Vol. 29, No.1 (January 2005), 15.

Gradually, however, Nilakanth distanced himself from Smith's evangelical conversion jargon to the more congenial conversion idiom of *ajñana* and *jñana*: from *ajñana* (ignorance and foolishness) to *jñana* (knowledge and wisdom). 'Thus, he began to remake himself in the image of a Benares pandit, transformed by *Christian* wisdom and called by God to make that wisdom *Indian* wisdom'. For Goreh 'there was no convergence between Vedanta and Christianity'. Goreh, states Young, was a Vaishnava *bhakta* whose *bhakti* 'was tinctured with Vedanta' and who admonished Vedantins 'to follow their hearts instead of their heads'.[23] Goreh was a Sanskrit scholar who did a careful comparative study of the Hindu and Christian religious systems.[24] Goreh believed that the religious systems of India were *praeparatio evangelii* (preparations for the gospel), provided by God in His providence to prepare Indians to accept Jesus Christ as the True Light.[25]

## Pandita Ramabai

It was Nehemia Goreh who filled an important role in Pandita Ramabai's spiritual quest. Partly due to their similar Marathi Chitpawan Brahmin background but also because of his sensitivity and appealing approach, Ramabai was able to interact meaningfully with Goreh. She wrote to him from England.

On the verge of becoming a Christian, Ramabai had doubts about certain aspects of Christian belief. In his reply, Goreh was able to settle her doubts as to the deity of Christ and other doctrinal issues, which enabled her to accept Christianity.[26] Goreh's writings

---

23 Young, 'Enabling Encounters: The Case of Nilakanth-Nehemiah Goreh, Brahmin Convert', *International Bulletin of Missionary Research*, Vol. 29, No.1 (January 2005), 14-18.

24 Aghamkar and Padole, *Christian Missions in Maharashtra*, 254-255.

25 Daniel Jeyaraj, 'The History of Christianity in India: An Overview from a Protestant Perspective' in *Missiology for the 21st Century: South Asian Perspectives* edited by Roger E. Hedlund and Paul Joshua Bhakiaraj, Delhi: ISPCK, and Chennai: MIIS, 2004, 205.

26 Aghamkar and Padole, *Christian Missions in Maharashtra*, 254-255.

gave Ramabai a solid foundation and model for defending her faith against those who attacked her. Ramabai's theological formation, the doctrinal and conceptual basis for her mission can be traced to Goreh's influence.[27]

## Narayan Vaman Tilak

Another significant convert was Narayan Vaman Tilak (1862-1919), Chitpawan Brahmin and famous poet of Maharashtra. Having grown dissatisfied with orthodox Hinduism, Tilak was given a New Testament to read. In the Sermon on the Mount he 'found answers to the most abstruse problems of Hindu philosophy'.[28] Convinced of the truth of Christianity, following a protracted period of mental conflict, in 1895 Tilak was baptized—but insisted that the ceremony be performed not by a foreigner but by an Indian.[29]

In her study of conversion in India, Gauri Viswanathan makes the point that while Tilak assimilated Christian beliefs and norms, he also 'sought to indigenize Christianity and make it compatible with Hinduism'.[30] P. S. Jacob points out that when Tilak joined the Christian Church he found that Christians in Maharashtra, due to their predominantly outcaste backgrounds, remained isolated from national life. This disability he set about to counteract using the instrumentality of his poetic works to instill love for India.[31] 'Tilak was strongly convinced that India's spiritual heritage is of great importance for expressing Indian Christianity'.[32] He utilized forms of

27 Aghamkar and Padole, *Christian Missions in Maharashtra*, 255.

28 J. C. Winslow, *Narayan Vaman Tilak: The Christian Poet of Maharashtra*, Third edition, Pune: Word of Life Publications, 1996, 20.

29 Eric J. Sharpe, 'Tilak, Narayan Vaman' in the *Biographical Dictionary of Christian Missions* edited by Gerald H. Anderson, New York: Simon & Schuster Macmillan, 1998, 671.

30 Gauri Viswanathan, *Outside the Fold: Conversion, Modernity, and Belief*, New Delhi: Oxford University Press, 1998, 40.

31 Palamthodathil S. Jacob, *The Experiential Response of N. V. Tilak*, Madras: CLS, 1979, 44.

32 Jacob, *The Experiential Response of N. V. Tilak*, 45.

Marathi spiritual literature to communicate the teachings of Christ. The devotional lyrics, music, poetry and prayers of Maharashtrian saints were effective vehicles to be adapted for Christian nurture and for developing the concept of Christian patriotism. In Tilak there was no conflict between nationalism and Christian faith. Patriotism is an aspect of Christian love. 'A Christian has to be a lover of his country'.[33]

Gauri Viswanathan interprets Tilak's conversion to Christianity as an assertion of anti-colonial Indian nationalism aiming for a revitalized India. 'Tilak conceived of Christianity as embodying a necessary vision of the future, with the power to purge Hinduism of its most hated caste features, yet at the same time adapted to India as a truly indigenous religion in its own right'.[34] To that end, he adapted Indian cultural forms such as the *bhajan* (Hindu devotional hymns) to Christian use.

An acknowledged Marathi literary figure, Tilak brought his poetic gifts to the service of Christ and the Church. Some 254 of his hymns are found in the Marathi hymnal.[35] In place of translated Western hymns, Tilak introduced the singing of *bhajans* and brought the use of *kirtan* into the Marathi Church, thus enriching its devotional life through familiar art forms—perhaps his greatest gift to the Christian Church. Tilak never gave up his Indian cultural birthright. He declared that he had come to Christ over the bridge of Tukaram, the Hindu poet-saint of Maharashtra. He brought the riches of his Hindu heritage into the Church.

Towards the end of his life he felt drawn toward *sanyasa*, and in 1917 became a Christian *sanyasi* determined to gather a brotherhood of baptized and non-baptized followers of Christ.[36] Tilak's devotional poetry, lyrics and hymns, represent 'a permanent treasury of devotion

33 Jacob, *The Experiential Response of N. V. Tilak*, 54.

34 Gauri Viswanathan, *Outside the Fold: Conversion, Modernity, and Belief*, 40.

35 Sharpe, 'Tilak, Narayan Vaman' in the *Biographical Dictionary of Christian Missions*, 671.

36 Robin Boyd, *An Introduction to Indian Christian Theology*, Madras: CLS, 1975, 115.

and theology for the Indian Church'.[37] Tilak hoped for India's conversion to Christ. Perhaps it was for that purpose that he wanted to move beyond the existing church. He left the employ of the Mission, and his home became a prototype of later Christian ashrams.[38] Tilak is considered a pioneer of the Christian ashram movement. *Khristacha Darbar* which he founded was an ashram community composed of both baptised and non-baptised disciples of Christ.[39] He embraced *sanyasa* as an Indian ideal and an appropriate channel for communicating the meaning of Christ. 'Tilak was certain that only in this type of Christian *sanyasa* could the true gospel of the true Christ be preached and win true disciples from among the Hindus'.[40] His practice of *sanyasa* was a renunciation of alien trappings in order to present Christ in familiar Eastern garb. 'He wanted to build an Indian Christian Church in truly Indian style and found it more suitable to become a Christian *sanyasi* for fulfilling this objective, rather than by continuing in the service of the Mission'.[41]

His inculturation of Christian faith also may have related to Tilak's second conversion. His first conversion was intellectual, the second, during middle age, was spiritual, 'a conversion of the heart rather than of the mind'[42] following which he became an exemplary Christian *bhakta* (a devotee in the *bhakti* tradition). No doubt Tilak was inspired by the *bhakti* traditions of Tukaram and the Maharashtrian saints. 'He applied the principles of *bhakti* to his newly found faith in Christ and did not find any conflict in this process of adaptation'.[43]

---

37 Robin Boyd, *An Introduction to Indian Christian Theology*, Madras: CLS, 1975, 117.

38 H. L. Richard, *Christ Bhakti: Narayan Vaman Tilak and Christian Work Among Hindus*, Secunderabad: OM Books, 1998, 61.

39 Aghamkar and Padole, *Christian Missions in Maharashtra*, 243.

40 Richard, *Christ Bhakti: Narayan Vaman Tilak*, 89.

41 P. S. Jacob, *The Experiential Response of N. V. Tilak*, 53.

42 Sharpe, 'Tilak, Narayan Vaman' in the *Biographical Dictionary of Christian Missions,* 671.

43 Jacob, *Experiential Response of N. V. Tilak*, 52.

As Robin Boyd observed, it was persons from the *bhakti* tradition who were best able to realize an Indian expression of Christianity.[44] Tilak's theology was Christocentric and experiential. The goal of *bhakti* was union with Christ leading to transformation through the power of the living Christ.[45] Like Tukaram, the poet saint of Maharashtra, Tilak was ever the religious poet and devotee. It was the treasure of the *bhajans* of the *bhakta* which Tilak brought to enrich the spiritual life of the Marathi Church. Tilak adapted a well-known Marathi Vaishnavite vessel into which he poured his devotion for Christ.[46] Through his poetry, Tilak expressed his love for India as well as his devotion to Christ.

It seems unfortunate that Hindu lovers of Marathi poetry tend to neglect Tilak's great work, apparently due to Tilak's religious conversion.[47] Anticipating his own death, Tilak instructed that his body should be cremated and that black should be avoided at his funeral. His wishes were respected, and it seems fitting that one of Tilak's own hymns was sung by the people during the funeral procession.[48]

Illustrious converts to Christ in the nineteenth century were predecessors of greater things to follow in the next century, particularly in the post-colonial era following independence.

44 Boyd, *An Introduction to Indian Christian Theology*, 114.

45 Jacob, *The Experiential Response of N. V. Tilak*, 20,23.

46 Malcolm Nazareth, 'Beyond the Pale of Colonial Discourse? Maharashtra's Christian Poet and Reformer', *Religion and Society* Vol. 44, No.3, September 1997, 62.

47 Ibid., 61.

48 Lakshmibai Tilak, *I Follow After: An Autobiography*, Delhi: Oxford University Press, Classic Reissue, 1998, 345.

Chapter 10

# North East India
# Here Come the Baptists

The growth and spread of Christianity during the nineteenth century provided the spring-board for accelerated expansion in the twentieth. At the same time, Christianity faced new challenges related to political events such as the 'Quit India' movement and eventual Independence. Partition and migrations were some of the new developments to be faced by newly Independent India. These developments had implications for the Churches and religious leaders. In this chapter, we will trace aspects of the further development of Christianity in India, a continuation of earlier developments, but with new entities to consider.

## North East India

North East India (NEI) is a case in point: earlier response among the Khasis, Manipuris, Mizos, Nagas and others continued together with new initiatives among tribal peoples of Assam and beyond. NEI is distinctive and important in the story of Christianity in India. Here, are the only states of India where Christians are a majority population, i.e., Nagaland (87.5% Christians), Mizoram (86% Christians), and Meghalaya (65% Christians). Manipur, in fourth place (34% Christians), is of special significance in that the hill area of the state is inhabited by tribals virtually all of whom are Christians, whereas the plains are inhabited mainly by non-tribals who are primarily non-Christians.[1] A similar pattern is found throughout North East India. Almost without exception the fiercely independent tribal peoples of NEI were never either Sanskritized nor Islamicized, yet today the vast majority are Christians as 'indigenously led conversion movements drew scores of separate tribal...peoples toward Christian faith in all of the eastern mountain frontiers'.[2] Today, the tribal populations of the seven NEI states are primarily Christian.

## Nagaland and Godhula

It will be of interest to have a closer look at the case of Nagaland. The gospel was first brought to the Nagas by an Assamese Christian by the name of Godhula. The people of Assam were terrified of the head-hunting Nagas. And the Nagas distrusted all strangers. Godhula first met an Ao Naga named Subongmeren who came down into the valley to barter. Godhula and his wife Lucy befriended Subongmeren and invited him to live in their home. There, Subongmeren absorbed essentials of the Christian faith, accepted the gospel and became a baptized believer.

Wanting his own people to know the redeeming love of God in Christ, Subongmeren asked Godhula and Lucy to consider coming up to his village. From Subongmeren, Godhula and Lucy learned as much as possible of the Ao Naga language. Finally, in October 1871 Godhula and Subongmeren began their perilous journey. Along the way they met other Ao Nagas who tried to dissuade Godhula,

1 Lalsangkima Pachuau, 'Church-Mission Dynamics in Northeast India' in *Missiology for the 21st Century: South Asian Perspectives*, edited by Roger E. Hedlund and Paul Joshua Bhakiaraj, Delhi: ISPCK and Chennai: MIIS, 2004, 214.

2 Robert Eric Frykenberg, *Christianity in India: From Beginnings to the Present*, New York: Oxford University Press, 2008, 421.

knowing they had no authority to bring a stranger into the village and could not vouch for his safety.

Arriving unannounced, Godhula immediately was taken into custody and placed in a small hut under armed guard. In his confinement, however, Godhula deployed a secret weapon: he began to sing. Nagas love music—especially vocal music—and Godhula had a good voice. Each day people came to listen, made friendly comments, and his fluency in the language improved. As numbers of hearers increased, he shared his faith, taught gospel truths, trying to connect Naga concepts and fears with biblical teachings. When Godhula was released and planned to return home, many of the Nagas wept and begged him to return and live with them.

Forty armed warriors escorted Godhula all the way back to Shibsagar.... And that was the beginning of the Baptist mission to the Nagas, pioneered by an Assamese Christian. Return to Molungkimong he did, several trips, and eventually with his wife Lucy became residents. The Nagas erected a bamboo chapel as a place of worship and learning. On 11 November 1872, nine newly-converted Ao Nagas were baptized and became 'the nucleus of the world's first Naga Christian congregation'.[3] Next month fifteen more believers were baptized, and the first Naga Baptist Church was born. By this time Godhula was joined by an American Baptist missionary, Dr. Edward Clark. Progress was not easy, there was opposition and danger. The steadfast courage of Godhula and Clark made a strong impression. The arrival of Clark's wife Mary further symbolized long term commitment.[4] The Christians decided to establish a new settlement, a 'village of refuge' to defuse tensions. Slowly transformation began. 'Christian communities became known as champions of peace'.[5]

3 Frykenberg, *Christianity in India: From Beginnings to the Present*, New York: Oxford University Press, 2008, 426.

4 Victor Hugo Sword, *Baptists in Assam: A Century of Missionary Service*, Chicago: Conference Press, 1935, 108-110.

5 Frykenberg, *Christianity in India: From Beginnings to the Present*, 431.

## Schoolhouse Christianity

The schoolhouse was the centre of the new village. Here, pioneer American Baptist missionaries, Edward and Mary Clark, 'laid the foundations of Naga literacy for the entire community'. An Ao Naga dictionary and grammar came into being using the Roman script. 'Literacy in their own mother tongue, together with literacy in English as a second language (and Assamese as a third), was like cultural dynamite. When whole villages became literate, this dynamite exploded, catapulting Nagas from the stone age into the modern world'.[6]

From the Ao Nagas Christianity spread to other tribes: the Angami Nagas, Lotha Nagas, Sema Nagas and others. In some cases, entire villages spontaneously turned Christian. Naga missionaries carried the message to unreached Naga tribes. Initially growth within the Ao Baptist Association was slow, then became more rapid after 1939. One by one, tribal church associations came into being among the Kuki, Rengma, Chakhesan, Zeliangrong, United Sangtam, Chang, Konyak, Phom, Yimchunger and Kheamungan tribes.

> 'Significantly, more Nagas turned Christian *after* the ending of imperial rule and the expulsion of foreign missionaries by the national Government of India. Nagas have resented charges that their faith was an alien implant upon hapless peoples.... Most conversions took place in districts well beyond spheres of missionary presence or colonial control'.[7]

Not surprising, then, Christianity is part of the Naga identity. Predominantly Baptist but also Catholic in at least one tribe, as well as Independent Charismatic in the Revival Church, the Nagas today participate in various local as well as global ecumenical and inter-church institutions and programmes. Theirs is an indigenous Naga Christianity.[8]

---

6 Frykenberg, *Christianity in India: From Beginnings to the Present*, 434.

7 Ibid., 443.

8 Ibid.

## A Complex History

The history of Christianity in the region is complex. Among the seven states ('Seven Sisters') of NEI, four are predominantly tribal and sometimes referred to as 'tribal states' namely Arunachal Pradesh, Meghalaya, Mizoram and Nagaland. With the exception of Arunachal, almost all the tribal people in the tribal states of Mizoram, Meghalaya and Nagaland are Christians. In the case of Manipur most of the hills tribes (comprising nearly half of the population of the state) are Christian, whereas the non-tribals of the plains region are predominantly non-Christian. With the exceptions of Arunachal Pradesh and Tripura, the tribal people of NEI are Christian and the non-tribals mostly non-Christian.[9] The Christian population of NEI amounts to about 23 percent of the Christians of India. Of the NEI states, Meghalaya has the largest number of Christians, roughly 1.2 million, followed by Nagaland with a million. Much of the growth has taken place during the 20th century, especially in the post-Independence era following the departure of the foreign missionaries.

The three largest denominations in NEI are the Baptists followed by the Roman Catholics and the Presbyterians. Baptist Churches of the Council of Baptist Churches in Northeast India (CBCNEI) dominate in Nagaland, in the Garo Hills of Meghalaya, in the Manipur hills, and in Christian pockets in the Brahmaputra Valley of Assam. The Catholics were mainly confined to Assam and Meghalaya until mid-century Independence following which the Catholic Church experienced explosive growth and has spread rapidly in other parts of the NEI region enjoying rapid growth in Manipur and Nagaland. The Presbyterian Church of India is dominant in the Khasi-Jaintia hills of Meghalaya as well as in northern Mizoram and in the Cachar district of Assam and in lesser numbers in the Manipur hills. The Baptist Church of Mizoram occupies southern Mizoram. Lutherans from Bihar/Jharkhand followed their migrant

9 Pachuau, 'Church-Mission Dynamics in Northeast India' in *Missiology for the 21st Century: South Asian Perspectives*, 213.

worker members and established Gossner Lutheran churches and Santal Mission outreach among tea garden labourers in Assam.[10]

Evangelization in North East India was carried out largely by the Christians of NEI. It was particularly so of Tripura and Arunachal Pradesh. Christianity was first brought to Tripura by Mizo Christian immigrants. Its remote location and difficult accessibility prevented Arunachal Pradesh from contact with the outside world including Christian missionaries but also impeded economic development. Beginning in the 1960s but increasing in the 1970s, there were conversions among the Adi and Nishi tribes. The Churches of NEI are animated for mission. 'Passion for mission is ingrained in the very lifeblood of the region's Christianity', states Lalsangkima Pachuau.[11] In Mizoram, the Presbyterian Church had 845 mission workers under the Presbyterian Church Synod as well as 182 Home Mission project missionaries, an aggregate total of 1027 Mizo Presbyterians engaged in missionary service in and out of Mizoram in the year 2002. That same year the Mizoram Baptist Church reported 418 mission workers outside as well as within Mizoram—working among non-Mizos. Some Mizo missions deploy missionaries to neighbouring countries, and others work in partnership with the Indian Evangelical Mission and other all-India mission agencies. In Nagaland, the Nagaland Missionary Movement represents the Nagaland Baptist Church Council, but most congregations tend to work independently or through their local tribal Baptist association. Churches of Manipur likewise are missionally active with as many as 576 workers deployed. Meghalaya has an estimated 350 mission workers under the Khasi-Jaintia Presbyterian Church as well as a number of missionaries sent from other denominations and Independent churches of the state.[12] Having experienced transformation, former head-hunters endowed with a sense of mission are spreading the salvific love of God beyond

10 Pachuau, 'Church-Mission Dynamics in Northeast India' in *Missiology for the 21st Century: South Asian Perspectives*, 215.

11 Ibid., 225.

12 Ibid., 226-228.

their own ethnic groups.[13] Churches in NEI are self-supporting as well as self-governing and self-propagating, animated by missionary zeal.

## Peace and Reconciliation

There is also a downside. Experience in the church as pastors, teachers, evangelists, interpreters and clerks meant that the Christians had acquired skills which could be deployed for service in the colonial bureaucracy. As Sujatha Fernandes states, 'Christian missionary activities provided the basis for the formation of a collegial society that could promote unity among tribes'.[14] Tribal leaders were developed who could articulate their concerns to the colonial state but also to the post-Independence Indian state.

Despite expressions of cross-denominational cooperation and unity, NEI has been marked by tribal and evangelical splintering, particularly in Manipur. 'Although evangelical Christianity promoted unity and brotherhood, its practical organization encouraged decentralization and supported the autonomy of individual tribal identities and cultures'.[15] This has played into the hands of militant organizations and separatist leaders fomenting communal violence in NEI. However, Christian leaders have tried to halt the process of fragmentation by introducing reconciliation events and appropriate tribal reconciliation ceremonies. 'Attempts at symbolic unity by church leaders play a very important role in promoting acceptance and reconciliation between the tribes'.[16]

---

13 O. L. Snaitang, 'Christianity as Social Transformation in North East India' in *Missiology for the 21st Century: South Asian Perspectives,* edited by Roger E. Hedlund and Paul Joshua Bhakiaraj, Delhi: ISPCK and Chennai: MIIS, 2004, 391.

14 Sujatha Fernandes, 'Ethnicity, Civil Society, and the Church: The Politics of Evangelical Christianity in Northeast India' in *Evangelical Christianity and Democracy in Asia* edited by David H. Lumsdaine, Oxford & New York: Oxford University Press, 2009, 137.

15 Ibid., 142.

16 Ibid., 146.

In a volatile environment the church has shown that it can play a peacemaker role. 'Evangelical Christianity has provided a forum through which tribals can express their political concerns and an idiom through which to frame their demands and concerns'.[17] An example is seen in a recent initiative for peace between two warring villages in the region. A joint pre-Christmas prayer service organized by the Assam Valley Baptist Mission (AVBM) brought together the leaders and members of two Baptist congregations, the Rajabari Baptist Church in Assam and Yajang-C village congregation in Mokokchung District, Nagaland, in a joint Christmas celebration at Rajabari Baptist Church. The president of the AVBM thanked both churches for organising the celebration and called for peace in the Assam-Nagaland border. Church members expressed their happiness, and it was hoped that the people of the two villages will take this peace initiative further.[18]

Clark Theological College (CTC) of Mokokchung, Nagaland, works closely with the AVBM in the peace initiative. A leadership training seminar conducted in May 2011 was attended by 50 pastors. The church in the region is comprised of Tea Estate workers and are poor in many ways. But, the fact is that churches are growing there and this is great news. There is often misunderstanding between Nagas and Assamese in the border area. The border peace coordination committee led by Er. Temsuwathi and other leaders from Assam has been working very hard during the last several years, and the efforts of the committee need to be recognised. Realizing the need to work for peace, CTC in 2011 inaugurated the Clark Centre for Peace Research and Action. Principal Dr. Takatemjen states, 'Our Peace Library is growing, and it has a collection of more than 1000 volumes that deal with peacemaking and conflicts in the

17 Sujatha Fernandes, 'Ethnicity, Civil Society, and the Church: The Politics of Evangelical Christianity in Northeast India' in *Evangelical Christianity and Democracy in Asia,* 151.

18 'Christmas celebrations ring in peace in NE region', posted by cninewsletter on December 20, 2011 in Indian News, available at: http://www.cathnewsindia.com/2011/12/20/celebrations-ring-in-peace-in-trouble-torn-ne-region/. Accessed on 21 December, 2011, 10:00AM.

region. We hope to do research on conflicts and peace-making in the Northeastern context through our MTh in Christian Ethics'.[19]

This gives further hope for dialogue and debate regarding issues of mutual concern between the multiplicity of Evangelical groups as well as non-Christian tribals in the region.

19 Takatemjen, E-mail correspondence to R. E. Hedlund, dated 26 December 2011.

Chapter 11

# Struggle for Survival
# Competence for Leadership

Not too far from the North East India region other tribal peoples are found who more recently have been turning to Christian faith. The Rabhas of West Bengal are such a tribal community. Linguistically part of the Bodo language group within the Tibeto-Burman language family, culturally close to the Bodo and Garo peoples, they are officially classed as Scheduled Tribes. The majority live in Assam with others settled in bordering states. The Rabhas of West Bengal belong to the Kocha section and commonly refer to themselves as Kocha.

## The Rabhas of West Bengal

Most Rabhas live within forest villages in the northern part of West Bengal near the Bhutan and Assam border, and it is here, since the late 1970s, that conversions have taken place. 'Today about two-thirds of the community are Christian and belong to the Rabha Baptist Church'. Why did the Rabhas chose to become Christians at this particular time in history? The Rabhas had been exposed to Christianity for at least a century but (with the exception of a few individuals) did not convert, whereas other tribals such as the Bodos did convert in large numbers at the end of the nineteenth and beginning of the twentieth centuries. Why now? Bengt Karlsson's carefully researched study concludes that the reasons given were largely pragmatic: 'The old religion had become both ineffective and too costly in today's world'. But there was also an implicit agenda of 'identity formation': 'By becoming Christian, a tribal community like the Rabhas could construct themselves as both different and modern. Their conversion was a form of 'cultural strategy' by which the community struggled to establish a new sense of self'. If so, the Rabhas' conversion to Christianity could be understood as part of a 'larger project of ethnic mobilization and a struggle for survival in the forest'.[1]

The Rabha story is important and needs to be told, and can help to correct a common misunderstanding which assumes the tribal converts to be victims of cultural imperialism. In contrast to that, Karlsson sees the people themselves (in this case the Rabhas) as competant agents who for various reasons 'choose to become Christians and make Christianity part of their own political and cultural projects and struggles'. From the first conversions onward, the expansion of the Rabha Baptist Church was a largely self-generating process. The villagers themselves invited the preachers to their villages, and Christianity spread from village to village. Sometimes, several families were baptized at the same time, but often it was an influential person who took the lead. When there are substantial numbers of Christians in a village, they form a congregation, elect officers and erect a building. Then the Baptist Union appoints an evangelist with special responsibility to educate the children. Few Rabha children attend school, and most Rabha can neither read nor write. The state schools are conducted entirely

---

1 Bengt G. Karlsson, 'Entering into the Christian Dharma: Contemporary "Tribal" Conversions in India' in *Christians, Cultural Interactions, and India's Religious Traditions* edited by Judith M. Brown and Robert Eric Frykenberg, Grand Rapids & Cambridge: Eerdmans Publishing, and London: Routledge Curzon, 2002, 139-140.

in Bengali, whereas the Baptist teachers use the Kocha language as the medium of instruction which is appealing to the Rabha. 'Many Rabha villages have become entirely Christian'. Education is one of the benefits offered through Christianity, providing competence for leadership in the modern world. Conversion is described by most Rabhas as 'a change to a new and better life' by which they enjoy 'a better standard of living', and Christians are seen as having become more 'developed'. Education is given high priority, and the same is true of the use of modern medicine. 'The only way for the Rabha to survive today, they say, is to become educated and to learn about the rights and the facilities available for their development'. Conversion for the Rabhas meant adopting a more appropriate way of life, a new *dharma* suitable for the modern world. 'Entering into the Christian *dharma* is indeed a serious matter....It is not so much a question of giving up one set of beliefs and adopting another new 'cosmology'. After all, most Rabhas know very little about Christian belief at the time of conversion. With the passage of time, as a person becomes active in the church, Christian beliefs and ideas will be grafted on to the old or previous ones. The dramatic change is instead...in the lifestyle or way of life of the convert'.[2]

From the Rabhas we learn that to change one's *dharma* is a matter of changing behaviour as well as of adopting new beliefs. For the Rabhas becoming Christian meant a radically new and better way of being Rabha.

## The Maltos of Jharkhand

We now turn to another tribal centre of North India, an area formerly known at Chotanagpur, now the state of Jharkhand. In a previous chapter we encountered the earlier Christianisation of several of the tribes in this area. Now, we come to consider the more recent turning to Christian faith of the Malto people of the Rajmahal hills of Jharkhand. Here, as in NEI the local Christians format their own

2 Karlsson, 'Entering into the Christian Dharma: Contemporary "Tribal" Conversions in India' in *Christians, Cultural Interactions, and India's Religious Traditions,* 142, 148, 149, 151, 153.

cultural adaptations of the Faith. Contrary to common presumption, it is not a ready-made Western type of church.

In a particularly lucid study of the movement into Christianity of the Maltos among whom he as a South Indian missionary has ministered for more than twenty years, R. George Edward traces the redemptive analogies which served as bridges for the gospel to enter and spread widely among the Maltos leading to positive worldview and lifestyle transformation.[3] At the time of George Edwards' writing, about 97 percent of the Maltos were illiterate, few villages had electricity, the people suffered from malaria and other water-borne diseases, infant mortality was high, population was in decline, and the tribe was demoralised by poverty, powerlessness and exploitation.

Analogies from Malto traditional religion were utilized by the Indian missionaries to communicate biblical concepts and practices. The Malto notion of *gosanyi* (God) was a starting point. Christianity shares the Malto belief in the existence of God as an all-powerful, everywhere-present and all-knowing Being. This Supreme Being, whom the Maltos thought to be distant and unknown, now is brought near and made known in the Lord Jesus Christ. The Malto practice of offering sacrifices for protection and provisions was a bridge to explaining the once-for-all sacrifice of Jesus Christ on the Cross.

> Every year Maltos sacrifice a buffalo, which they consider the greatest sacrifice to please *gosanyi* [God] and to seek blessings and protection from the spirits. This sacrifice shares some similarities with the Christian concept of Christ's sacrifice on the cross, though the Christian God no longer expects animal sacrifice. Maltos also offer sacrifices to propitiate harmful spirits. Similarly Christ's death propitiated God and so reconciles humans with God. The idea of sacrifice

3 R. George Edward, 'Modern People Movements: A Jharkhand Case Study' in *Missiology for the 21st Century: South Asian Perspectives,* edited by Roger E. Hedlund and Paul Joshua Bhakiaraj, Delhi: ISPCK and Chennai: MIIS, 2004, 430-445.

has helped the animist Maltos to understand the meaning of reconciliation with God.

In Malto belief the shedding of blood in sacrifice brings peace from *gosanyi.* This belief is very similar to the biblical teaching that the shedding of Christ's blood on the Cross was for the forgiveness of sin (Hebrews 9:22). Rituals are important in Malto traditional religion, and many traditional customs have been retained with some modifications as needed. Some, Christian rituals have been introduced such as harvest festivals, communion services, Bible verse competitions, festivals of the Holy Spirit, fasting prayer, all night prayer, church dedications, house dedications, child dedications, memorial services and thanksgiving services. These provided bridges to make Christ known and to meet the Malto felt need for ritual. The Maltos believe in the existence of evil, and live in constant fear of evil spirits. The proclamation of Christ as Victor over demons and Saviour from evil came as wonderful Good News. Miracles and healings in Jesus' name serve to make Christ known as the Almighty Lord. 'Power encounters have played an important part in the spread of Christianity among the Maltos'. Traditionally, the Maltos had no concept of life after death and consequently no hope. But the preaching of the gospel awakened hope for the after-life, peace instead of fear, trust in place of dread, 'a new life of fullness and hope, a new spiritual life for the Malto community as a whole and for every Malto individual'. Indian cross-cultural missionaries, recognising the significance of the mother tongue for effective communication, used the heart language of the Maltos knowing that 'Maltos prefer to hear the gospel preached in Malto rather than in Hindi or Santali'. The missionaries also utilized convenient Malto customs and practices. The Malto custom of washing feet in welcoming guests was related to Jesus' washing his disciples' feet (John 13). The Malto love of singing was recognised, and their own kind of music utilized for gospel presentation and teaching. Sensitivity to Malto ideas and practices helped build bridges of understanding. Today, transformation of the

Maltos is a growing reality with Malto literature and improved living conditions symbolic of their new found dignity in Christ.[4]

## Dangs, Gujarat

Far from Jharkand in the North and Bengal in the East, on the opposite side of the Indian subcontinent in Gujarat are found a number of pockets of tribal populations.

One such is the Dangs, the smallest district of Gujarat, bordered by Dhule and Nasik districts of Maharashtra and Surat and Valsad districts of Gujarat, heavily forested and about 93.5% tribal. The Bhils are the original inhabitants, the Kuknas and Varlis and a few Ganuts and Choudhris came later from adjoining areas to cultivate the land. All these tribes over a period of time have forged a common Dangi identity of social structure, norms, customs, culture and language — some 84 percent speak Dangi.[5] From the early nineteenth century onward devastation of Dangi forest resources has undermined tribal social structure and impoverished the inhabitants. Encroachment and loss of livelihood drove the *adivasis* into a cycle of debt and dependency on nontribal merchants and unscrupulous moneylenders. Terms of interest were rapacious: one and a half times with compound interest to be repaid at harvest—guaranteed to perpetuate impoverishment—some were forced to work as slaves to repay debts.

This is the context into which indigenous South Indian missionaries entered in the 1970s. The missionaries serve sacrificially and with great zeal, animated by the example of the great Indian Bishop V. S. Azariah 100 years ago whose model of itinerant evangelism and pastoral care by indigenous Christians they seek to emulate. The austere lifestyle of the missionaries helps to gain

---

4 George Edward, 'Modern People Movements: A Jharkhand Case Study' in *Missiology for the 21st Century: South Asian Perspectives*, 431, 433-434, 438-439, 443.

5 Sushil J. Aaron, 'Emulating Azariah: Evangelicals and Social Change in the Dangs' in *Evangelical Christianity and Democracy in Asia* edited by David H. Lumsdaine, Oxford & New York: Oxford University Press, 2009, 93.

the confidence of the *adivasis*. In addition to evangelism, today the Mission engages in community development, medical and agricultural assistance and educational projects. The Mission seeks ways to respond to particular needs such as extensive alcohol abuse. 'Deliverance from alcohol addiction ranks next to healing as a cause for allegiance to Christianity, particularly among women, who readily accept Christ after their husbands give up drinking'. Use of the vernacular languages by the missionaries has served to enhance the respectability of the tribal languages which is further enhanced through literacy and Bible translation—'a fair measure of cultural recovery for the tribals'.

In this and other ways Evangelicalism has challenged abusive power structures and contributed to positive self-awareness among the *adivasis*. 'It is enabling Dangi *adivasi* greater access to opportunities, resources, and equality, particularly in overcoming hindrances to respect and fair treatment. It also provides ways for them to engage the increasing incursions of modernizing and globalizing India without simply being increasingly marginalized and displaced'.[6] This may explain why Evangelical Christianity is viewed as a threat by those who profit by exploiting the *adivasis* and other vulnerable sectors of society.

## The Vasava

In 1974, the Friends Missionary Prayer Band (FMPB), an indigenous mission from South India, began ministry in Gujarat and have worked among 13 tribes in eleven states of North India.[7] Among them the Vasava people of the Sathpura hills were particularly responsive. The Vasava are a sub-sect in the Bhil tribal belt, mainly landless cultivators. The FMPB missionaries learned the Vasava dialect and

6 Sushil J. Aaron, 'Emulating Azariah: Evangelicals and Social Change in the Dangs' in *Evangelical Christianity and Democracy in Asia,* 93-95, 100, 109-110, 118.

7 The information which follows is drawn from the FMPB commemoration of 25 years among the Vasava, *The Vasava Church: History with Signs and Wonders,* Chennai: Friends Missionary Prayer Band, 2005, 18-42.

prepared literacy materials in the previously unwritten language, prepared a book on Vasava phonetics and published the first few books in Vasava. By October 2004, translation of the Vasava New Testament was completed and handed over to the Bible Society of India for publication. Young men and women as well as church elders were taught biblical truths and learned how to conduct meetings and *bhajans*. Initially classes were conducted in believers' homes, sheds or rented buildings, but eventually a Leadership Training Institute emerged with its own facilities where local evanglists, church elders, teachers and social workers are trained. Many social programmes have developed including children's homes, an adult literacy programme, health programmes including a small hospital, clinics and medical camps, vocational training, self-help groups with income-generating jobs and an English school for Vasava and other children.

Miracles, signs and wonders are prominent including deliverance from demonic possession and disease, barrenness and destitution. 'Largely because of these miracles, the Church could take root in the cross-cultural context'. A compendium of miracles and wonders documents cases of healing, protection, and provision of food and other needs as answers to prayer. In May 2004, the FMPB formally handed over to the Church of North India 207 congregations formed by FMPB missionaries including 55 from the Vasava area, with 10,000 believers participating in the function.[8]

Christianity was found attractive to various tribal and Dalit peoples of India during the twentieth century, increasingly so in the years following independence. As we shall see, India continues to make its own distinct contributions and imprints on World Christianity.

8 *The Vasava Church: History with Signs and Wonders,* 44, 43-96, 97.

Chapter 12

# Indian Christianity
## Pentecostal, Evangelical and Ecumenical

Not to be overlooked in an overview of Christianity in India is the emergence of the Pentecostal movement during the twentieth century. The modern Pentecostal movement is thought by many to have originated at the famous Azusa Street revival (1906-1908) in Los Angeles. That assumption however overlooksearlier Holy Spirit revivals in India as well as in other parts of the world.

### Mukti Mission & Pandita Ramabai

A year prior to the Azusa Street event, a Holiness revival with accompanying charismatic manifestations began (1905-1907) at Pandita Ramabai's Mukti Mission in Kedgaon near Pune. The revival at Mukti Mission in 1905 is looked upon by some scholars as a beginning point for Indian Pentecostalism. 'Ramabai is both significant in the origins of Pentecostalism and in the acceptance of its phenomena among some in the wider Christian community'.[1]

1 Allan Anderson, '"The Present World-Wide Revival... Brought Up in India": Pandita Ramabai and the Origins of Pentecostalism' in *Indian and Christian:*

According to Allan Anderson, 'Ramabai's life resonates with Pentecostal images and experiences'.[2] Ramabai's initial intellectual conversion to the truth of Christianity was followed years later in 1896 by an intense spiritual awakening, which she described as 'the personal presence of the Holy Spirit in me'.[3] Perhaps her experience is best understood in Wesleyan-Holiness terms as an experience of sanctification. Ramabai was in contact with Methodist Holiness in the person of Miss Minnie Abrams as well as with the Deeper Life emphasis of Keswick. From this further conversion stems Ramabai's evangelical identity combining intense spirituality with a vigorous social engagement. Her interest in Keswick Holiness brought openness to the subsequent revival movement with accompanying Pentecostal manifestations. Pentecostal religious experience shows affinity to the *bhakti* expressions of the devotional Hinduism in which Ramabai was nurtured. The mystical tradition is common in both. Edith Blumhofer's cryptic comment seems fitting: 'Without ever becoming a Pentecostal in the Western sense of the term, Ramabai played a significant role in the spread of Pentecostalism'.[4]

In 1898, Ramabai addressed the Keswick Convention in England where she requested prayer for an outpouring of the Holy Spirit in India. It was around this time that Ramabai heard about revival in Wales (U.K.) and about a revival conducted by R. A. Torrey in Australia. To the latter in 1904 she dispatched her daughter, Manoramabai, and Minnie Abrams to observe and bring a report. As an outcome of their visit, in January 1905 Ramabai instituted voluntary daily early morning prayers for the true conversion of all

---

*The Life and Legacy of Pandita Ramabai,* edited by Roger E. Hedlund, Sebastian Kim & Rajkumar Boaz Johnson, Delhi: ISPCK, Chennai: MIIS, 2011, 308.

2 Anderson, 'Pandita Ramabai and the Origins of Pentecostalism', 311.

3 Anderson, 'Pandita Ramabai and the Origins of Pentecostalism', citing Rajas K. Dongre & Josephine F. Patterson, *Pandita Ramabai: A Life of Faith and Prayer*, Madras: Christian Literature Society, 1963, 18, 24, 72-3.

4 Edith L. Blumhofer, 'Consuming Fire: Pandita Ramabai and the Early Pentecostal Impulse' in *Indian and Christian: The Life and Legacy of Pandita Ramabai,* edited by Roger E. Hedlund, Sebastian Kim & Rajkumar Boaz Johnson, Delhi: ISPCK, Chennai: MIIS, 2011, 151.

Christians and for an outpouring of the Holy Spirit. The number at this morning retreat gradually increased from seventy women to more than five hundred. In July 1905, a revival began which lasted for a year and a half resulting in significant transformation: confession of sin, repentance, hundreds of girls going out as preaching teams into the surrounding areas.[5] The Mukti revival is looked upon as one of the points of origin of the Pentecostal movement in India.[6]

## Prior Revivals in India

As is pointed out by A. C. George and others, Pentecostal-like movements began in South India at Tirunelveli and Travancore nearly fifty years before the revival at Mukti. Kerala experienced three major revivals in 1873, 1895 and 1905 in which glossolalia (speaking in tongues), healings and visions were reported.[7] That Pentecostal missionaries soon made their way to India from Azusa Street attests to the missionary character of the Pentecostal movement, it does not negate the importance of revivals with Pentecostal phenomena in India prior to the arrival of Western missionaries. One such was the ministry of John Christian Arulappan in the 1860s, which recorded 'explicitly Pentecostal features'.[8] There were others as well. According to Pentecostal historian Gary McGee, 'the most prominent revivals

5 Anderson, 'Pandita Ramabai and the Origins of Pentecostalism', 311-312.

6 'Indigenous Pentecostalism in India' by Roger E. Hedlund in *Asian and Pentecostal: The Charismatic Face of Christianity in Asia* edited by Allan Anderson and Edmond Tang, Oxford: Regnum Books, and Baguio City: APTS Press, 2005, 215-244, which, however, requires correction of a factual error on page 215: Minnie Abrams at that point in time [when she joined Ramabai at Mukti Mission] was a Methodist missionary from America, of Holiness persuasion, but not yet a Pentecostal.

7 A. C. George, 'Pentecostal Beginnings in India', *Dharma Deepika* July-December 2002, 43.

8 Paulson Pulikottil, 'Emergence of Indian Pentecostalism', *Dharma Deepika* July-December 2002, 48.

of the nineteenth century characterized by the charismatic gifts of the Holy Spirit occurred in India'.[9]

## Prominent South Indian Leaders

Missionaries from the West inevitably generate publicity, which unfortunately (if unintentionally) obscures the essential contributions of local Christian leaders. In the second decade of the twentieth century this changed with the emergence of gifted South Indian leaders such as Ramankutty Paul, K. E. Abraham, P. M. Samuel and K.C. Cherian who established Pentecostal churches under their own leadership.[10] 'These leaders took the Pentecostal faith to the rest of South India and were the founding fathers of the Pentecostal Faith in Tamil Nadu, Andhra Pradesh, and parts of Karnataka'.[11]

## South Indian Pentecostalism

The first major scholarly study of South Indian Pentecostalism touches the history of all known Pentecostal bodies in South India and lists a total of 71 Pentecostal bodies in the four southern states.[12] Andhra Pradesh has 14 Pentecostal denominations, Karnataka seven and Kerala eleven, but Tamil Nadu has the greatest number with 33 Pentecostal denominations. This is not an exhaustive listing as new groups frequently appear, and inevitably researchers and enumerators miss some groups. A similar investigation in North India would reveal parallel developments of new Pentecostal and Charismatic bodies in Mumbai, Delhi, Punjab and Uttar Pradesh. A common thread running through these Churches is a conscious expression of their Indian identity and character. Their Pentecostal

---

9 An unpublished article by Gary B. McGee, ca 1999, cited by A. C. George, 'Pentecostal Beginnings in Travancore, South India', *Asian Journal of Pentecostal Studies* 4/2 (2001), 220.

10 Paulson Pulikottil, 'Emergence of Indian Pentecostalism', *Dharma Deepika* July-December 2002, 52.

11 Ibid., 53.

12 Michael Bergunder, *The South Indian Pentecostal Movement in the Twentieth Century*, Grand Rapids & Cambridge: Eerdmans Publishing, 2008.

faith unites them with fellow-believers worldwide. At the same time, an indelible 'Indianness' marks their habits of life and culture. Their expressions of Indian Christian nationalism deserve commendation and respect.

Some of the new so-called 'small churches' do not remain small. In Chennai, for example, the mother church of the Apostolic Christian Assembly (ACA), a notable movement of indigenous origin, attracts more than 13,000 worshipers to its Sunday morning bi-lingual service.[13] In addition there are at least 144 ACA branch churches in India with a total of 17,600 believers.[14] Also in Chennai, the New Life Assembly of God at Tenempet attracts more than 33,000 worshipers to its multiple weekend services every Saturday and Sunday. In Mumbai, the New Life Fellowship is a vigorous urban movement that has grown to several thousand members found in more than 300 house churches and 500 house groups plus 140 prayer cells and 122 composite celebration centres in rented facilities throughout the city.[15]

## Kerala

In Kerala, a number of early South Indian Pentecostal leaders were Thomas Syrian Christians who, having served as leaders in the Brethren movement, now moved into the Pentecostal fold, in some cases bringing with them their congregations. So, it is not surprising that they became leaders in the Pentecostal movement.[16] Four main Pentecostal bodies began during the 1920s and '30s, namely the Assemblies of God, the Ceylon Pentecostal Mission, the Church of God and the Indian Pentecostal Church of God. The capable

13 This was observed during my visits on 13 February and 1st April, 2000, and confirmed in interviews with Pastor Sam Sundaram on 30th March and with Pastor Kumar on 1st April, 2000, at Chennai.

14 Apostolic Christian Assembly, *Annual Report, 1996-1997*, Chennai, 1997.

15 Information was provided by the lead pastors whom I interviewed at the home of the founder, Pastor S. Joseph, at Mahim, Mumbai, on 26 February 1998. Growth has continued.

16 Ibid., 30.??? = original source???

leadership of the Thomas Christians no doubt is an important factor contributing to Pentecostal growth, although a domineering leadership style might also have inhibited growth.[17] Dalits were sensitive to caste discrimination practiced by some Pentecostal leaders.[18] In his study of Dalit Pentecostalism in Andhra Pradesh, Rapaka indicates that it was the sacrificial living, steadfast faith and endurance of suffering of Dalit pastors which contributed to the growth of the IPC in Andhra.[19] The Dalits had hoped to achieve higher social status in Pentecostalism, but this goal was shattered by the prejudicial leadership of Syrian Christians who regarded the Dalits as inferior and treated them as Untouchables.[20] It is not surprising that new institutions and churches came into being due to 'the inability of the churches led by the Thomas Christians to integrate Dalit or Nadar leaders'.[21] Sharon Fellowship and Faith Theological Seminary, New India Church of God, New India Bible Church and New India Bible College, Gospel for Asia and the Believers' Church, Church of God in Kerala and the Church of God (Division) and Zion Sangham are among newer Pentecostal entities in Kerala who in various ways accommodate Dalit and Nadar leadership and concerns.[22]

---

17 Ibid., 30.??? = original source???

18 V. V. Thomas, *Dalit Pentecostalism: Spirituality of the Empowered Poor* (Bangalore: Asian Trading Corporation, 2008), 235, cited by Yabbeju Rapaka, 'The Indian Pentecostal Church of God in Andhra Pradesh, 1932 to 2010: A Study of Dalit Pentecostalism', PhD Dissertation, School of Divinity, Regent University, September 2011, 67.

19 Rapaka,'The Indian Pentecostal Church of God in Andhra Pradesh, 1932 to 2010: A Study of Dalit Pentecostalism', PhD Dissertation, 101.

20 Ibid., 73-74.

21 Bergunder, *The South Indian Pentecostal Movement,* 54.

22 Ibid., 50-56. See also Alexander Philip, 'Selected Indigenous Church Movements in Kerala: A Study' in *Christianity is Indian: The Emergence of an Indigenous Community* edited by Roger E. Hedlund, Delhi: ISPCK and Chennai: MIIS, revised 2004, 291-317.

## Tamil Nadu

In Tamil Nadu, significant Pentecostal bodies include the Assemblies of God, Church of God, Indian Pentecostal Church, Ceylon Pentecostal Mission, Full Gospel Pentecostal Church, Pentecostal Church of India, Apostolic Christian Assembly, Apostolic Fellowship Tabernacle, Maranatha, Madras Pentecostal Assembly, Kirubasanam, Jehovah Salvation Church, Indian Pentecostal Assemblies, Indian Christian Assembly, Full Gospel Pentecostal Church and Trinity Full Gospel Church as well as other fellowships, Bible schools, and independent churches.[23]

## Karnataka

In Karnataka in the city of Bangalore, the Assemblies of God denomination is the strongest Pentecostal presence, and its Southern Asia Bible College (SABC) the leading Pentecostal training institution in South India. Also, in Bangalore the Nava Jeeva Ashram founded by Dr. John Thannickal is an attempt to stimulate a contextual proclamation of the gospel through adaptation of the Indian *guru-shishya* principle. Other Pentecostal-Charismatic initiatives include the Gospel Prayer Hall, Shekinah Gospel Prayer Fellowship, Christian Fellowship Centre and various local congregations in Bangalore but also in Kolar Gold Fields and other outlying areas of the state.[24]

## Andhra Pradesh

The story of Pentecostalism in Andhra Pradesh is somewhat complex involving the establishment of local centres of the Indian Pentecostal Church of God whose registration took place at Eluru in Andhra Pradesh, rather than in Kerala, resulting in a somewhat decentralized structure. A local branch created in Vijayawada in 1940 by P. M.

23 Bergunder, *The South Indian Pentecostal Movement*, 58-85.

24 Ibid., 86-90. On Pentecostalism at Kolar Gold Fields see Siga Arles, 'Indigenous Pentecosal Church Growth at Kolar' in *Christianity Is Indian: The Emergence of an Indigenous Community* edited by R. E. Hedlund, Delhi: ISPCK and Chennai: MIIS, revised 2004, 385-398.

Samuel established Samuel as the IPC leader in Andhra, and also provided a proto-type for other cities. Also in 1940 P. T. Chacko established a local centre in Secunderabad but maintained close ties to Kerala through the marriage of his daughter to T. S. Abraham, son of the IPC founder K. E. Abraham. T. S. Abraham thereafter spent half the year in Kerala and the other half in Andhra. In 1942 P. L. Paramjothi arrived in Antarvedipalem to strengthen the IPC in the Godavari Delta and became a significant leader of the IPC in that area.[25] Eventually the IPC was to evolve into something like a union of small denominations.[26]

Other Pentecostals in Andhra Pradesh include the Assemblies of God: in 1978 Gera Peter started a Telugu Bible school; in 1983 American missionary Earl Stubbs began an English-language church in Hyderabad; and in 1984 Gera Peter began systematic church planting.[27]

An interesting development in Andhra is the role of expatriate Non-Resident Indians (NRIs) returning to India to found churches and institutions. Among them Ernest Komanapalli founder of the Rock Church in Hyderabad and leader of Mana, an umbrella organization for a variety of projects including 45 orphanages, a home for lepers, ten schools, two junior colleges and a hospital. 'By the 1990s Komanapalli had become the most influential Pentecostal leader in Andhra Pradesh'.[28] Another NRI, P. J. Titus, in 1982 returned to India to establish the Church on the Rock Theological Seminary (COTR) which according to Bergunder soon became 'one of the most important educational institutions for the Indian Pentecostal movement'.[29]

25 Bergunder, *The South Indian Pentecostal Movement*, 92-94.

26 Ibid., 211.

27 Ibid., 100.

28 Ibid., 100-101.

29 Ibid., 101.

## Response to Popular Hinduism

Indian Pentecostalism is not without its challenges. During the 1980s, the arrival of the 'Faith Movement' brought an amount of dissonance but was generally rejected along with the 'prosperity gospel'. Nevertheless, Bergunder found that the books of Kenneth Hagin and Yonggi Cho are read by many pastors. 'To assure oneself of God's blessing in this world is a general leitmotif of Pentecostal spirituality in south India'.[30] Bergunder contends that South Indian Pentecostalism is not a copy of Western models but that rather it has come to terms with popular Hinduism especially in its outlook as to causes of misfortune such as illness, untimely death, infertility, family strife, failure in business or profession, or any kind of bad luck.[31] Evil spirits are believed to be the responsible cause of these misfortunes. In popular Hindu thinking evil spirits (*pêy, picâcu*) are the spirits of those who died 'bad' deaths, i.e., prematurely or through misfortune. If and when these evil spirits 'possess' someone they cause diseases and all kinds of trouble. The only solution then is exorcism, and this is where Pentecostal worldview responds to popular Hindu beliefs and practices. In Bergunder's understanding, 'the Pentecostals have taken over the demonology of popular Hinduism, with some slight differences'.[32] Indian Pentecostalism is not captive to the skepticism and rationalism of the West. With a vernacular Bible as their guide, Pentecostal healers and evangelists practice exorcism, anoint the sick with oil, pray for healing and protection from evil spirits. Among South Indian Pentecostals, 'exorcism is an essential part of pastoral and evangelistic practice'.[33]

## Northeast India

In Northeast India a 1905 revival in the Presbyterian Church is attributed to the impact of the 1904 revival in Wales. Manifestations

30 Bergunder, *The South Indian Pentecostal Movement,* 122.

31 Ibid., 123.

32 Ibid., 125.

33 Ibid., 147.

included spontaneous collective prayer, singing, dancing, trembling, shouting and being 'slain in the spirit'. If speaking in tongues occurred, it was not reported. Nevertheless, in the opinion of historian O. L. Snaitang, this revival might be considered a harbinger of the rise of Pentecostalism in Northeast India.[34] Bergunder likewise affirms that events in the Khasi Hills (as well as at Mukti Mission) played an important role in the worldwide revival that took place in the first decade of the twentieth century.[35]

In Meghalaya the indigenous Church of Jesus Christ—Full Gospel, formed in 1932, grew rapidly and has spread throughout the region. Emphasis on the authority of the Bible in its doctrine and practices, vibrant worship, speaking in tongues, and deliverance ministries are familiar Pentecostal-Charismatic practices. A distinctive feature particularly appealing in a matrilineal society is this Church's decision to ordain women. At its Assembly meeting at Tynghor in March 1952, the Church ordained Mrs. Gratissimo Ryntathiang, the first ordained woman in all of India as well as in the Northeast.[36]

In Mizoram indigenous Christianity comprises a variety of charismatic, revival, prophetic and Pentecostal elements which fit well with the traditional culture. Manipur is a region of many tribes in which Pentecostal and other Independent churches appear to form along separate ethnic lines of identity. Revival in Nagaland brought new spiritual vitality to the churches, which touched the lives of church members and also brought in new converts. When the revival movement clashed with official church leadership, the revivalists formed new independent congregations from which in 1962 emerged the Nagaland Christian Revival Church (NCRC), an indigenous Pentecostal movement. Other Pentecostal churches from outside the state came to Nagaland only after the formation of the NCRC.The Pentecostal-Charismatic movement has grown rapidly

34 O. L. Snaitang, 'The Indigenous Pentecostal Movement in Northeast India', *Dharma Deepika* July-December 2002, 7.

35 Bergunder, *The South Indian Pentecostal Movement*, 23.

36 Snaitang, 'The Indigenous Pentecostal Movement in Northeast India', *Dharma Deepika* July-December 2002, 7-8,

in the hill areas of Meghalaya, Mizoram, Nagaland and Manipur, but is yet to find a significant following in Assam, Arunachal Pradesh, Sikkim or Tripura.[37]

## Pentecostal Missionary Movement

The modern Pentecostal movement began as a missionary movement! Even before the formation of the first Pentecostal denomination, Pentecostal Christians were engaged in missionary sending.[38] Pentecostal fire, ignited at Azusa Street, Los Angeles, in the first decade of the twentieth century, spread rapidly to the ends of the earth. The Pentecostal Revival took seriously the command of Christ to evangelize the world.[39] Within 100 years the Pentecostal-Charismatic movement has grown to become the second largest body of Christians, larger than all other Protestants, exceeded only by the Roman Catholics. In India, today the Pentecostals comprise the fastest growing section of the Church, and the Charismatic Movement has a growing impact in the Roman Catholic Church. The largest Protestant congregations in Bangalore, Chennai and Kolkata are Pentecostal. In Mumbai, the New Life Fellowship is a rapidly multiplying Charismatic urban house church phenomenon. These churches are actively engaged in various social programmes which benefit the poor and marginalized.

## Pentecostal Theology

Pentecostal theology is essentially a theology of the Acts of the Apostles. The baptism, gifts, and fruit of the Holy Spirit are for Christian character building and are essential for the ministry of the Church and for carrying out mission. The indigenous church

37 Snaitang, 'The Indigenous Pentecostal Movement in Northeast India', *Dharma Deepika* July-December 2002, 9-10.

38 Gary B. McGee, *This Gospel Shall Be Preached: A History and Theology of Assemblies of God Foreign Missions to 1959*, Springfield, Gospel Publishing House, 1986.

39 See L. Grant McClung (ed.) *Azusa Street and Beyond: Pentecostal Missions and Church Growth in the Twentieth Century*, New York, Bridge Publishing, 1986.

principles of Melvin Hodges facilitate lay initiative and leadership innovation. Pentecostal ecclesiology encourages the ministry and training of the laity. The Pentecostals provide a participation model for developing local leadership in the living situation.[40]

The dominant theme of the Book of Acts is 'the expansion of the church through missionary witness in the power of the Holy Spirit'.[41] The Pentecostal approach takes seriously the problems of spirit possession and demonic manifestations. A missiology of power rather than mere argument and intellect is both revolutionary and relevant. Pentecostal missiology postulates a theology of the Kingdom. 'The Kingdom in pneumatological terms has to do with the witness of the Church in the Spirit's power and the universalization of mission under His direction'.[42] Pentecostals, the poor, and phenomenal church growth are linked together because of the disposition of the poor toward repentance and faith by which they enter the Kingdom.[43] The Holy Spirit as the Advocate of Jesus Christ is central in this redemptive activity.

Pentecostal theology seems particularly suited to the task of mediating the message of Christ among the majority communities of South Asia. The witness of the laity, a willingness to live by faith, the disciplines of fasting and prayer, deliverance ministries and miraculous healings all serve to authenticate the message of Christ.[44] Pentecostal theology is relevant in India.

---

40 Lesslie Newbigin, 'Theological Education in a World Perspective' in *Missions and Theological Education in World Perspective,* edited by Harvie M. Conn and Samuel F. Rowen, Farmington, Michigan, Associates of Urbanus, 1984.

41 Paul A. Pomerville, *The Third Force in Missions: A Pentecostal Contribution to Contemporary Mission Theology*, Peabody, Hendrickson Publishers, 1985, 72.

42 Pomerville, *The Third Force in Missions,* 150.

43 Ibid., 152-153.

44 P. T. Abraham, 'Indigenous Cross-Cultural Missions in India and Their Contribution to Church Growth: With Special Emphasis on Pentecostal-Charismatic Missions', Ph.D. dissertation, Fuller Theological Seminary, 1990.

Chapter 13

# Indian Christianity
## Ecumenical, Contextual and Catholic

The twentieth century was an era of worldwide ecumenical developments such as the birth of the World Council of Churches (WCC) inaugurated in 1948 at Amsterdam. India has been an active participant in the WCC through several member Churches. The 3rd WCC Assembly took place in New Delhi in 1961. For a number of years M. M. Thomas of the Mar Thoma Church served as Moderator of the WCC Central Committee.

### Ecumenical Developments

India is regarded as an ecumenical 'showcase' because of two significant events. These were the formation of the Church of South India (CSI) in 1947 and the Church of North India (CNI) in 1970. CSI in particular is celebrated as the historically first-ever union of Episcopal and non-episcopal Churches.[1] Some 28 years of deliberations preceded the merger in which four historical traditions

1 Ninan Mathew, 'Church of South India, a brief History', available at http://www.csichurch.com/article/ninan.htm , Accessed on 20th December, 2011.

(Anglican, Congregational, Methodist, Presbyterian) agreed to become one united Church. CNI represents an even broader union consisting of Anglican, Baptist, Church of the Brethren, Congregational, Disciples of Christ, Methodist and Presbyterian Churches joining together as one united/uniting Church. CSI and CNI are important ecumenical milestones, rightly celebrated as significant Indian achievements.

There was an earlier platform, which also ought not be forgotten.

## Indigeneity and Catholicity

High Anglicans in the Church of England had always carried a concern for the *catholicity* of the Church by which they meant not only its unitary oneness but its apostolic origins which they traced to Christianity's first century, concerns shared and expressed in India by the Society for the Propagation of the Gospel (SPG) and the Society for the Promotion of Christian Knowledge (SPCK).

Evangelicals of the Church Missionary Society (CMS)—also Anglicans—were, however, much more concerned for the spread of the gospel and the development of Indian churches than for a 'territorial episcopacy' which implied 'Anglicizing' and connoted a spread of 'Englishness'.[2] Henry Venn, the Honorary Secretary of the CMS and its greatest missiological theorist, had long promoted the concept of indigeneity for which the development of a plurality of national or 'native' churches was indicated. Had Venn's vision prevailed, a robust 'Native Church of India' might well have developed under indigenous clergy but without colonial bishops.[3]

---

2 C. Peter Williams, 'The Church Missionary Society and the Indigenous Church in the Second Half of the Nineteenth Century: The Defence and Destruction of the Venn Ideals' in *Converting Colonialism: Visions and Realities in Mission History, 1706-1914*, edited by Dana L. Robert, Grand Rapids & Cambridge: Eerdmans Publishing, 2008, 89.

3 Ibid., 90-91.

## Inculturation in the Catholic Church

Similar tensions are discernable in the Catholic Church in India when Eurocentric norms are imposed without consideration of local cultures and values. 'This fact creates an ambiguity and suspicion among the Asians who otherwise are deeply attracted to Christ and His message'.[4] Leaders complain that the Indian Church is not given authority to make needed changes, and that issues are decided by persons lacking cross-cultural experience and insight. Inculturation is not a matter of inserting Brahmanical elements into the liturgy, but of interpreting anew the message of Christ according to the tribal, Dalit and folk cultures of India as well as the Sanskritic cultures of the elite. Inculturation must seek the incarnation of the Church in the life and sufferings of all the excluded in their struggles for human rights and dignity.[5]

## Independent Churches

New independent churches, it is said, grow at the expense of older established congregations. That is one side of the story. A former bishop, now demised, commented that the so-called mainline churches have become almost stagnant with disillusionment among their own members, whereas the newer 'small missions and indigenous churches' led by charismatic leaders are thriving.[6] When the older denominations are preoccupied with property disputes and struggles for power, spiritual values are lost. It is not surprising then, if church members gravitate to the newer independent churches where fresh

4 Joseph Mattam, 'The Message of Jesus and Our Customary Theological Language: An Indian Approach to a New Language in Theology and Inculturation' in *Sharing Diversity in Missiological Research and Education* edited by L. Stanislaus and John F. Gorski, Pune: Ishvani Kendra, Delhi: ISPCK, 2006, 51.

5 Ibid., 52-54.

6 P. Victor Premasagar, 'Are Indigenous Churches A Silent Protest against the so-called Mainline Churches?' Appendix Two in *The New Wine-skins: The Story of the Indigenous Missions in Coastal Andhr Pradesh, India* by P. Solomon Raj, Delhi: ISPCK and Chennai: MIIS, 2002.

winds of the Spirit of God are blowing. Here are to be found a caring community engaged in ministry to the sick, concern for a holy and ethical lifestyle, and expectations for visible answers to prayer.[7]

These new churches deserve to be known and understood, perhaps as expressions of popular folk religion. They consist of lesser known churches and recent new movements of Indian origin. They are important and should be studied along with the better-known traditional Churches.[8] In his study of the new Christian movements, Solomon Raj affirms their validity and vitality as Indian expressions of historic Christian faith, and provides a list of 19 Bible schools and colleges functioning mainly in Hyderabad training leaders for the churches of the 'Little Tradition' in Andhra Pradesh, many of them practicing a *guru-sishya* type of learning as well as classroom lectures.[9]

## Indian Christology

Christianity in India has always existed alongside other religious traditions. The resulting interaction has enriched the form and substance of Christian theology, and Christianity has made an imprint upon other faiths. In various ways 'Hinduism and Buddhism have undergone renewal as a result of being confronted with a missionary Christianity'.[10] Translation of the gospel into new cultural settings has been a primary avenue for discovering new insights. 'Historically it has been the diverse religious-cultural

7 P. Solomon Raj, *The New Wine-skins: The Story of the Indigenous Missions in Coastal Andhra Pradesh, India*, Delhi: ISPCK and Chennai: MIIS, 2002, 125.

8 Roger E. Hedlund, 'The Importance of the Study of India's New Christian Movements', Appendix One in *The New Wine-skins: The Story of the Indigenous Missions in Coastal Andhra Pradesh, India* by P. Solomon Raj, Delhi: ISPCK and Chennai: MIIS, 2002.

9 Solomon Raj, *The New Wine-skins*, 74.

10 David M. Thompson, 'Introduction: mapping Asian Christianity in the context of world Christianity' in *Christian Theology in Asia* edited by Sebastian C. H. Kim, Cambridge: Cambridge University Press, 2008, 130-150.

complexes Christianity has encountered, that have been the primary contexts for theological development'.[11]

Christian theology arising from a Hindu context will bear distinctive marks of its context. Antony Kalliath points out that before Christian theologians began to think about Indian Christology, Hindus like Vivekananda, Ramakrishna, Keshub Chunder Sen and Mahatma Gandhi had already appropriated Jesus and developed a Christological spirituality—an experiential Christology and a vibrant Christophany among non-Christians![12]

Indian Christology takes form in a context of poverty in which millions struggle for basic necessities of life. The uniqueness of the Cross distinguishes Jesus from Buddha or Krishna, and identifies Jesus with the multitudes of poor and suffering. This is the reality in which a large number of Hindus as unbaptized *Jesubhaktas* (devotees of Jesus) accept Jesus as Lord and Guru.[13]

## Inculturation and Dialogue

Indian Churches inculturate in a variety of ways including adaptation of local customs and rites deemed suitable for Christian worship, communication and life.[14] Preaching in an Asian mode can utilize song and poetry, drama, short story, apocalyptic and word play which are rich in Asian cultures; yet this is where many fall short and hence

---

11 S. Mark Heim, 'Witness to Difference: Missions and the Religions in Post-Pluralist Perspective' in *News of Boundless Riches: Interrogating, Comparing and Reconstructing Mission in a Global Era,* Vol. I, edited by Max L. Stackhouse and Lalsangkima Pachuau, Delhi: ISPCK, Bangalore: UTC, and Princeton: Centre of Theological Inquiry, 2007, 103.

12 Antony Kalliath, 'Liberative Dialogue Towards Harmony of Life: Interrogating Catholic Missiology in a Futuristic Perspective' in *News of Boundless Riches: Interrogating, Comparing and Reconstructing Mission in a Global Era,* Vol. I, edited by Max L. Stackhouse and Lalsangkima Pachuau, Delhi: ISPCK, Bangalore: UTC, and Princeton: Centre of Theological Inquiry, 2007, 82-84.

13 Ibid., 71.

14 M. Thomas Thangaraj, 'Religious pluralism, dialogue and Asian Christian responses' in *Christian Theology in Asia* edited by Sebastian C.H. Kim, Cambridge: Cambridge University Press, 2008, 159-163.

fail to reach an impoverished oral audience in which video games and television have replaced reading.[15] An example of inter-religious dialogue is seen in a recent Interfaith *Satsang* organized at Ishvani Kendra in Pune bringing together representative leaders of Islam, Sikhism, Jainism, Buddhism, Hinduism and Brahma Kumaris as well as Christians around the theme of 'Religions for Peace' in which the Staff of Ishvani Kendra, an SVD-run Institute of Missiology and Communications, shared the peace and joy of Christmas with the followers of other religions.[16]

'Religions should promote peace', stated Bishop Thomas Dabre in welcoming the representatives of the different faiths at Pune. Then added, 'Let peace begin with each one of us'.[17] The Pune event is an example of the religions coming together on a common platform to promote religious harmony and social well-being. Another recent instance was an inter-religious seminar in New Delhi convened by the Catholic Bishops' Conference of India, the Archdiocese of Delhi and the world fellowship of religions in which Christians and Jains were urged to promote their common concerns for the sanctity of life and its protection. 'Christians and Jains have many things in common', stated Cardinal Jean-Louis Tauran of the Pontifical Council for inter-religious dialogue, 'our vocation to promote respect for life, non-violence, peace and harmony in today's world brings us together with the common bond of mutual affection for each other'.[18]

---

15 See *Naming the Unknown God* edited by Adonis Abelard O. Gorospe, Manila: OMF Literature and Quezon City: Asian Theological Seminary, 2006.

16 Joy Thomas joythomassvd@gmail.com(For details of the Interfaith Satsang, visit: www.ishvanikendra.com <http://www.ishvanikendra.com/> and www.svdinm.org <http://www.svdinm.org/> ). Accessed on 21/12/11.

17 Priscilla Pinto, 'Religions should promote peace, says bishop'; available at http://www.cathnewsindia.com/2011/12/20/inter-faith-meet-emphasizes-on-restoring-peace-human-dignity/. Accessed on 22/12/11.

18 Ritu Sharma, 'Promote culture respecting human life' posted by cinenewsletter on November 14, 2011 in Indian News; available at http://www.cathnewsindia.com/2011/11/14christian-jains-have-much-in-common-cardinal-tauran/. Accessed on 22/12/11.

## Southward Tilt

India today is part of the southward tilt of world Christianity.[19] As Lamin Sanneh explains, world Christianity is 'the movement of Christianity as it takes form and shape in societies that previously were not Christian'.[20] 'The new world situation for the Christian religion demands a new history of Christianity', states historian Mark Noll.[21] More believers gathered for Sunday worship in Nagaland than in Norway, India now home to the largest chapter of the Society of Jesus (Jesuits)—these are some of the facts.[22] Of course, the case for the new paradigm promoted by Philip Jenkins[23] and others ought not be over-stated. As Robert Wuthnow reminds us, with the exception of the Pentecostals, 'much of the apparent growth of Christianity in certain parts of the world is simply the result of high fertility'.[24] So be it. The vitality of the Christianity of the southern hemisphere is cause for joy and gratitude to Almighty God for new possibilities for theologizing together and for creative new partnerships in leadership training,[25] in providing humanitarian aid, for growth in mutual

19 See Dana Robert, 'Shifting Southward: Global Christianity Since 1945', *International Bulletin of Missionary Research* April 2000, 50-58.

20 Lamin Sanneh, *Whose Religion is Christianity? The Gospel beyond the West*, Grand Rapids & Cambridge: Eerdmans Publishing, 2003, 22.

21 Mark A. Noll, *The New Shape of World Christianity*, Downners Grove: IVP Academic, 2009, 9.

22 Ibid., 10.

23 Many have written about aspects of the new southward centre of Christianity, none more than Philip Jenkins. See: *The Next Christendom: The Coming of Global Christianity*, New York: Oxford University Press, 2002; *The New Faces of Christianity: Believing the Bible in the Global South*, New York: Oxford University Press, 2006; *The Lost History of Christianity: The Thousand-Year Golden Age of the Church in the Middle East, Africa, and Asia—and How It Died*, New York: Harper One, 2008; and other titles.

24 Robert Wuthnow, *Boundless Faith: The Global Outreach of American Churches*, Berkeley: University of California Press, 2009, 44, 59.

25 Leon P. Spenser, 'Not Yet There: Seminaries and the Challenge of Partnership', *International Bulletin of Missionary Research*, Vol. 34, No. 3 (July 2010), 150-154.

understanding and acceptance. Christians in India are known as a peaceful community, and it is not uncommon for public officials to express appreciation for Christian contributions to society especially in education, health and social services.[26]

India today, in the early decades of the twenty-first century, is an important contributor in the development of World Christianity.

26 Catholic News India, available at http://www.cathnewsindia.com/2011/12/22/maharashtra-cm-lauds-christian-contribution-to-society/. Accessed on 26/12/2011.

Chapter 14

# A New Era of World Christianity[1]

The ancient Thomas Christianity of India had faced challenges but also experienced renewal through its encounter with a succession of other Christian traditions making their way to India. These have included Eastern Nestorians, Latin Catholics, Pietist Protestants and Pentecostal Charismatics as we have seen. Each of these has made an impact in India, more importantly Christianity has been enriched by India. The rubric 'World Christianity' is used by Lamin Sanneh, Andrew Walls and others to capture the dynamic and diverse expressions of Christianity rooted not in Western globalization but in the vitality and variety of local renditions of Christian faith worldwide but especially in Africa, Asia, Latin America and the Pacific.[2]

1 Portions of this chapter appeared in a paper, 'Challenges to Mission in the 21st Century', presented as part of the Tambaram IMC Platinum Jubilee (1938-2013) at Madras Christian College, Chennai, 13-14 December 2013.

2 Lamin Sanneh, 'Post-Western Wine, Post-Christian Wineskins? The Bible and the Third Wave Awakening' in *Understanding World Christianity: The Vision and Work of Andrew F. Walls* edited by William R. Burrows, Mark R. Gornik, and Janice A. McLean, Maryknoll: Orbis Books, 2011, 92.

## World Christianity

World Christianity celebrates the universality of Christianity as a translated religion, which places God at the centre of human cultures all of which become potential bearers of the Word of God through Bible translation. 'The rapid, unprecedented expansion of Christianity from the second half of the twentieth century has thrown into high relief the impact of Bible translation on societies beyond the West and exposed the limitations of post-Christian wineskins in the face of new ferment'.[3] The word 'World' tells us that 'Christianity is no longer the religion of the West but a world religion'. Theologically 'world' links Christianity to the catholicity and apostolicity of the Church, i.e., its continuity, universality and authenticity. 'Christianity is about the transformation of individuals and communities as they embrace Christ and direct their lives and cultures toward God'. What we believe about God, about Christ and the Church makes a difference. Catholicity embraces a wide range of Christian diversity, and apostolicity relates that diversity to the historic confession of Christian faith as handed down to us generation by generation from its earliest custodians and sources. Thus 'theology and ecclesiology cannot avoid the responsibility of judging what is genuine and what is spurious'.[4] 'World Christianity' displays the cultural diversity, which expresses 'the real identity of Christ in ways never experienced before'-- referred by Walls as the 'fortunate subversion of the Church' that will lead to new expressions of theology, mission and vulnerability.[5] 'For Andrew Walls, the story

3 Sanneh, 'Post-Western Wine, Post-Christian Wineskins? The Bible and the Third Wave Awakening' in *Understanding World Christianity: The Vision and Work of Andrew F. Walls*, 99,103.

4 William R. Burrows, 'Conversion: Individual and Cultural' in *Understanding World Christianity: The Vision and Work of Andrew F. Walls* edited by William R. Burrows, Mark R. Gornik, and Janice A. McLean, Maryknoll: Orbis Books, 2011, 122-123.

5 Stephen B. Bevans, 'Ecclesiology, Andrew F. Walls, and the Fortunate Subversion of the Church' in *Understanding World Christianity: The Vision and Work of Andrew F. Walls* edited by William R. Burrows, Mark R. Gornik, and Janice A. McLean, Maryknoll: Orbis Books, 2011, 127. See also Andrew F.

of World Christianity is that of Christianity as a non-Western religion with multiple local manifestations'.[6] Walls experienced the resurgence of Christianity through its grassroots growth and diversity in Africa, and his scholarly formulations are informed by that experience and from the lessons of history. Yet underneath it all is a biblical and theological foundation: 'the Revelation vision of Jesus' followers, called out from every tribe and nation, sustains his commitment to the existence of Christianity as a worldwide faith'.[7]

## Non-Traditional New Churches

World Christianity is non-Western, innovative and venturesome. In India a degree of bold innovation is notable among numbers of non-traditional new churches. Precedence was found in earlier examples such as the Punjabi mystical devotee Sadhu Sundar Singh (1889-1929) who preached in many churches but appears to have never been closely attached to any.[8] Also from Punjab, Brother Bakht Singh (1903-2000), evangelical follower of Jesus Christ, evangelist, Bible-centred preacher and founder of Jehovah Shammah at Madras (Chennai) and more than 200 local assemblies throughout India characterized by Bible teaching, devotional singing, testimonials, and worship manifesting cultural similarity to practices adapted from the Gurdwaras of Punjab and from the Bible.[9] Contemporary

---

Walls, 'Missionary Societies and the Fortunate Subversion of the Church', in *The Missionary Movement in Christian History: Studies in the Transmission of Faith*, Maryknoll: Orbis Books, 1997, 247.

6 Dana L. Robert, 'Historiographic Foundations from Latourette and Van Dusen to Andrew F. Walls' in *Understanding World Christianity: The Vision and Work of Andrew F. Walls* edited by William R. Burrows, Mark R. Gornik, and Janice A. McLean, Maryknoll: Orbis Books, 2011, 152.

7 Ibid., 153.

8 Biographies of Sundar Singh are many. See Eric J. Sharpe, *The Riddle of Sadhu Sundar Singh*, New Delhi: Intercultural Publications, 2004; A. J. Appasamy, *Sundar Singh*, Cambridge: Lutterworth, 1958; C. F. Andrews, *Sadhu Sundar Singh: A Personal Memoir*, New York: Harper & Brothers, 1934; and others.

9 The definitive biography is by T. E. Koshy, *Brother Bakht Singh of India: An Account of 20th Century Revival*, Secunderabad: OM Books, 2003. Also 'The

Pentecostalism in the early 21st century offers a variety of independent churches and denominations. In Chennai, a number of monthly gatherings of pastors cluster around several prominent personalities. All night prayers are not uncommon among evangelicals in South India, and certain Pentecostal evangelists also organize similar events.

A major novelty was Sadhu Chellappa's use of Hindu scriptures to try to convince Hindus (and Christians) that Christ is found in Hindu texts. In the recent past the late D. G. S. Dhinakaran attracted huge crowds to his healing crusades and became 'the best-known and most successful evangelist in the whole of India'.[10] In South India, a succession of popular evangelists continue to attract a wide following, and the Charismatic movement has greatly influenced most major Protestant denominations as well as the Roman Catholic Church.[11] In a study of new Christianity in Chennai, Pradip Ninan Thomas expresses disappointment that mainline Churches have failed to counter the 'Christian fundamentalists' who are attracting Indian Christian youth from the older traditional Churches.[12] Christian worship has been Americanized throughout India, states Thomas, and neither the new churches nor the old-line denominational churches offer praise and worship based on the styles of Hindu devotional hymns (*bhajans*) and use of *tabla*, *harmonium* and traditional Indian instruments.[13]Cultural change is inevitable, and

---

Bakht Singh Movement' by Moses Premanandam in *Christianity Is Indian: The Emergence of an Indigenous Community* edited by Roger E. Hedlund, Delhi: ISPCK and Chennai: MIIS, revised 2004; and Roger E. Hedlund, *Quest for Identity: India's Churches of Indigenous Origin*, Delhi: ISPCK and Chennai: MIIS, 2000, 152-156, 175-179.

10 Michael Bergunder, *The South Indian Pentecostal Movement in the Twentieth Century*, Grand Rapids & Cambridge: Eerdmans Publishing, 2008, 108.

11 Ibid., 107-129.

12 Pradip Ninan Thomas, *Strong Religion, Zealous Media: Christian Fundamentalism and Communication in India*, New Delhi: SAGE Publications, 2008, xvi, 139.

13 Ibid., 99.

some of today's popular 'fads' may soon pass into oblivion. There is a deeper concern.

## Charismatic Televangelism

The 21st century witnessed the advent of Charismatic televangelism in India and with it subtle changes in the worship of the church, the style and content of preaching, and patterns of ministry. In his study of the phenomenon, Jonathan James finds that Charismatic televangelism has an impact both on the Protestant Church and on the Hindu community. An example is seen in the Benny Hinn 'Festival of Blessings' three-day Crusade at Mumbai in February 2004, "one of the largest events in the history of Indian Christianity" reportedly attended by 4.2 million people—despite the fact that Hinn had never previously visited the Indian subcontinent. Hinn's Florida-based megachurch, however, had been 'broadcasting his healing and teaching programmes through satellite television to India for at least six years before he set foot on Indian soil'. The question arises whether televangelism might constitute a new phase of Christian outreach in India, driven by Americans, with little or no cultural adaptation?[14] Global Charismatic television has had an indelible impact upon both Protestant Christianity and the Hindu community in India.

James concludes that Christianity in India may never be the same. Protestant missionaries of the past such as Ziegenbalg at Tranquebar and William Carey at Serampore respected the local cultures and followed an indigenous approach. By way of contrast, 'McDonaldisation' and 'Masala McGospel' describe the Americanization of Indian Christianity through television. James' research reveals that in the past Christianity thrived when rooted in the local indigenous culture, expressing respect for the Hindu social system and meeting the needs of converts. Hindu-Christian tensions increased when Christianity was not adequately indigenized to the

14 Jonathan D. James, *McDonaldisation, Masala McGospel and Om Economics: Televangelism in Contemporary India*, New Delhi: SAGE Publications, 2010, xvii, xviii-xix, xxii.

culture. With the rise of *Hindutva,* tensions are likely to intensify. 'Western forms of evangelism, Western fundsand structures seem to exacerbate the growing tensions between Hindu nationalistic groups and the Christian church'.[15] About 85 percent of Christian television in India originates in USA, Britain and Australia. Only 10 percent of the programmes are locally produced in India, and about 90 percent of these are by K. P. Yohanan, Sam Chelladurai, the late Brother Dinakaran, and other well-known Indian Charismatics.

Charismatic televangelism in India is 'reinventing' Christianity contends James. The 'reinvention' takes place through 1) a new charismatic hermeneutic, 2) a new theology of communication with television the embodiment of the Holy Spirit, 3) a new set of teaching and practices centered in healing, deliverance, prosperity and success, 4) a new clergy, and 5) a new electronically mediated liturgy.[16]

Christian leaders are concerned lest the outcome be a Christianity without Christ and without participation in the life of the local church. *Hindutva* advocates react with an agenda of anger and vow to 'promote the idea that Christianity is the greatest threat to national harmony, security and sovereignty'. In light of this threat, James's counsel for the Church in India 'to become as fully indigenous as possible' seems entirely appropriate.[17]

## *Isa*-Muslims and Christ *Bhaktas*

There is, however, another development, a movement, which goes beyond the translatability of Christianity as deliniated by Andrew Walls and Lamin Sanneh.[18] A recent scholarly study of the transformation of Christianity focuses on two groups that confessed explicit faith in Jesus as Christ, disassociated themselves from

15 James, *McDonaldisation, Masala McGospel,* 98, 90.

16 Ibid., 184, 190-197.

17 Ibid., 171, 206, 209.

18 See especially the ground-breaking study by Lamin Sanneh, *Translating the Message: The Missionary Impact on Culture*, Maryknoll: Orbis Books, 1989, as well as other writings on 'translatability' by Sanneh and by Andrew Walls.

Western Christianity, and continue as 'marginal religious groups in the border-lands between Christianity, Islam and Hinduism'. 'With their self-understanding and hybrid identity as *Isa*-Muslims and *Khrist bhaktas*-Hindus, their faith relation to Jesus transcends the traditional denominational boundaries of Christianity'.[19]

The study of the *Isa*-Muslims at Dacca shows 'how faith in Jesus Christ is experienced, expressed, and apprehended through Islamic and Bengali concepts' that through extensive translation result in an indigenous Christianization. In the case of the Christ-*Bhaktas* in Chennai, 'the translation of faith in Jesus Christ takes place through a number of elements from Hindu *bhakti* religiosity which is brought into the Christian theological universe. As a result, the *bhaktas* become devotees at the 'feet of Christ' and Jesus is seen as the source of salvation and knowledge. The *bhaktas'* faith is thus experienced and expressed through common Hindu concepts', i.e., their faith is centred on Christ but utilizes Hindu aspects to better comprehend the meaning of Christ.[20]

It will be helpful to recall that the brilliant and devoted follower of Christ, Pandita Ramabai (1858-1922), at no time reviled her Hindu heritage and regarded herself as both Hindu and Christian.[21] A double affiliation of the more recent Christ *bhaktas* likewise is not novel or surprising. Their common Indian-ness is an important asset. To retain what is 'Indian' the *bhaktas* reinterpret Hindu rituals, which they combine with Christian symbols and practices. These include baptism as *diksha*, communion as participating in Jesus' *maha prasad*, singing of *bhajans* to Jesus, and use of coconuts, incense, and flowers in worship, thus giving new meaning to existing rituals and forms. According to their own explanations, the *bhaktas* give new Christian meaning to existing Hindu rituals and forms. 'Just as the

19 Jonas Adelin Jørgensen, *Jesus Imandars and Christ Bhaktas: Two Case Studies of Interreligious Hermeneutics and Identity in Global Christianity*, Frankfurt: Peter Lang, 2008, 1-2.

20 Ibid., 8.

21 See several essays is the recent symposium, *Indian & Christian: The Life and Legacy of Pandita Ramabai*, edited by Roger E. Hedlund, Sebastian Kim and Rajkumar Boaz Johnson, Delhi: ISPCK and Chennai: MIIS, 2011, 76.

first disciples were Jewish believers in Christ, the *bhaktas* perceive themselves as *Hindu believers in Christ*'.[22]

One might recall the well-known Bengali convert of a century ago, Brahmabandhav Upadhyay (1861-1907), who joined the Catholic Church, but preferred to call himself a Hindu Catholic or Hindu Christian, adapted and used Vedantic language in order to re-state Christian theology in terms better understood in India and thereby provided an indigenous philosophical base for Indian Christianity.[23] The *satsang* (fellowship meetings) of the Christ-*bhaktas* resemble similar Hindu gatherings led by a *guru* (teacher) who mediates divine truth to the devotees, and the use of *bhajans* (devotional hymns) as suitable for approaching the divine. Moreover the incorporation of these 'Hindu' or Indian elements takes place in a 'Christ-centred' worship and theological setting. The Christology of the Christ-*bhaktas* places them *outside* the Hindu theological system, for they understand Jesus Christ as the *incarnate* absolute.[24] The *bhaktas* 'place themselves within the Christian theological universe through their Christology', which amounts to an enlargement of Christian meaning through 'a translation of Hindu concepts and symbolizations' into Christian theological use and practice. If so, in Jørgensen's opinion, the result is a new form of Christianity, a 'Hindu Christianity'. Heresy? Perhaps, but theological tension might be a better term. By taking refuge in Jesus, the *bhaktas* have shifted their allegiance to the feet of Jesus as their source of salvation. 'If there is a Hindu way of being Christian, the *bhaktas* come close to such a form of religious life and in the process they "enlarge" the Christian theological universe'.[25]

---

22 Jørgensen, *Jesus Imandars and Christ Bhaktas: Two Case Studies of Interreligious Hermeneutics and Identity in Global Christianity*, 395.

23 Timothy C. Tennent, *Building Christianity on Indian Foundations: The Legacy of Brahmabandhav Upadhyay*, Delhi: ISPCK, 2000, 360, cf 10, 224.

24 Jørgensen, *Jesus Imandars and Christ Bhaktas: Two Case Studies of Interreligious Hermeneutics and Identity in Global Christianity*, 397-398.

25 Ibid., 404, 406.

## *Khrist-Bhaktas* of North India

*Khrist-bhaktas* are found not only in Chennai, but also in locations in North India with minimal Christian presence or exposure. One such place is Varanasi. The Roman Catholic bishop of Varanasi, the Most Rev. Patrick D'Souza, tells of a recent movement in which thousands are coming regularly to request teaching about Jesus and to join in Christian prayers. 'On an average they spend four hours with us every week. They read the Gospels, they want our guidance in reading the Bible, in prayers of thanksgiving and petition'.[26] They are from other religions, they are unbaptized, but they want to know Jesus. It seems to be a spontaneous movement without any human agent, surely 'a movement from the Holy Spirit', states the Bishop. The *bhaktas* are neither baptized nor registered. There has been no opposition;'the movement is spreading by the people speaking about it to one another'.[27]

Theologian George Praseed clarifies that the *Khrist Bhakta* Movement (KBM) began in 1993 when the Matridham Ashram of Varanasi opened its doors to the Charismatic Movement.The devotees belong to a variety of castes and professions, the majority are women, and predominantly from the lower strata of society. The movement provides 'opportunity for people of all castes to gather together, pray, and sing loudly in the open'. Those who have found healing and peace in their families through prayers to Jesus, in turn, bring others to the movement. The KBM has grown to outnumber the Catholic population of Varanasi Diocese and has spread to nine districts of eastern Uttar Pradesh, some districts in western Uttar Pradesh, and to a few of the districts of Bihar.[28]

26 Patrick D'Souza, 'Devotees of Christ' in *Co-Worker for Your Joy:* Festschrift *in honour of George Gispert-Sauch S.J.* edited by S. Painadath and Leonard Fernando, Delhi: Vidyajyoti College and ISPCK, 2006, 227.

27 Ibid., 230.

28 George Praseed, 'Khrist Bhakta Movement' in the *Oxford Encyclopaedia of South Asian Christianity*, edited by R. E. Hedlund, J. M. Athyal, J. Kalapati and Jessica Richard,Oxford University Press, New Delhi, 2011, 373-374.

In today's globalized world, it is inevitable for Hindu devotees of Christ to appear among the South Asian diaspora in the West. The testimonial of one K. Venkatesh reveals a combination of many factors: a strict high caste Hindu family, opportunity to study in an American university where he met Christians, tragedy in his family in India, love and support of Christians during this family crisis, reading the New Testament, decided to pray to Jesus, the next day the crisis began to resolve, and 'before long the matter had been settled'. Venkatesh continued to read the New Testament and soon came to believe in Jesus.

Venkatesh later returned to India where he is very much part of the Hindu community. Because of his academic qualifications and standing in the community, people listen to him. There are many discussions about Jesus, and he shares the Bible with many in the community. Venkatesh explains: 'Now I have quite a few friends who are also following Jesus, and we meet regularly to pray together and share the Scriptures and to encourage each other.'[29] In reading the New Testament, he had observed that Jesus never spoke about the Christian religion but only spoke about following Him. This is the experience of many in India who are attracted to Jesus, but continue to have doubts about the Christian church. And this quandary has occasioned considerable debate.

## Churchless Christianity?

The late Lesslie Newbigin, former bishop in the Madras Diocese of the Church of South India, is one who engaged in published debate with the well-known Indian ecumenical figure M. M. Thomas about the latter's over-spiritualization of ecclesiology which fails to resolve the clash between one's ultimate loyalty to Jesus Christ and one's dual identity as a Hindu. Church as Newbigin understood it must involve a visible community, whereas some advocates of a Churchless

29 K. Venkatesh, 'Living and Discipling in the Hindu World', *Mission Frontiers* May-June 2011, 17.

Christianity appear willing to dispense with the church as a visible entity.[30]

In a review of the Churchless Christianity concept, theologian David Wells reminds us that 'there was always an inescapable corporate dimension to believing' and 'that there are vital aspects of the Christian experience which simply cannot be had alone, disconnected from the people of God'.[31] Newbigin and others who share his outlook agree that faith in Christ will eventually require visible, social forms. 'There will inevitably be points where a tension will develop which requires a faithful, public response'.[32] Responding to Tennent, H. L. Richard declares, 'New corporate expressions of public discipleship to Jesus within Hindu cultures and communities certainly do not need the label "Christian," nor do they need any particular kind of relationship with existing "Christian" churches and denominations'. In rebuttal, Tennent's final comment is that 'one cannot maintain Hindu religious identity and at the same time be a follower of Jesus Christ – Catholicity implies that we identify ourselves with other followers of Christ'.[33] And so the debate continues.

## Seekers for Truth

An alternative 'third' way is wanted which will embrace the merits of both of the above viewpoints without denying the catholicity, historicity and *missional* nature of the church. A 'missional' church will be 'oriented to the world' and also 'true to its identity as an agent of God's mission and a participant in God's story'.[34] As William

30 See Herbert E. Hoefer, *Churchless Christianity*, Madras: Gurukul Lutheran Theological College & Research Institute, 1991.

31 David Wells on 'Churchless Christianity' available at http://www.reformationtheology.com/2006/08/david_wells_on_churchless_chri.php ; accessed on 2nd December 2011.

32 Timothy C. Tennent, 'A Response to H.L. Richard's Community Dynamics and the Praxis of "Church",' *International Journal of Frontier Missiology* 24:4 Winter 2007, 196.

33 Ibid., 197.

34 Michael W. Goheen, *A Light to the Nations: The Missional Church and the Biblical Story*, Grand Rapids: Baker Academic, 2011, 5. Also see Craig Van Gelder (ed.)

Burrows adds, 'Precisely in order to be faithful to its identity, a church must always be in reformation to the extent that it confronts situations different from those in which it was originally founded'.[35] In India, today we need to recapture the vision and mission of the famous Methodist evangelist E. Stanley Jones (1884-1973) who 'by living his faith in the midst of religious pluralism, he focused on the centrality of Christ'.[36]

Through the centuries India has had reformers who brought a message of hope and renewal; among them are Kabir (1440–1518), Jyotiba Phule (1827-1890) and Ambedkar (1891-1956) as well as others. Maharashtrian social reformer Jyotirao Phule is of particular interest because of his initiatives to educate women and the lower castes. Phule organised the first *Satya Shodhak Samaj* (Society of Seekers of Truth).

Phule was the father of the Truthseeker movement. It was Phule who first connected the Indian character of Baliraja to Christianity's Jesus. This is still the message that Truthseekers International is bringing to the lowered castes in India. Truthseekers points to the writings and teachings of Phule when relating Baliraja to Jesus because the people already know the story of Baliraja.[37]

The contemporary Truthseekers International, started in 2003 by Sunil Sardarand his wife Pam, derives its name and model from Phule's *Satya Shodhak Samaj*. It is self-described as 'A Christ-Centered Reconciliation Movement' seeking to communicate a

---

*Confident Witness—Changing World*, Grand Rapids & Cambridge: Eerdmans Publishing, 1999, and other titles in the Missional Church movement.

35 William R. Burrows, 'Witness to the Gospel and Refounding the Church' in Craig Van Gelder (ed.) *Confident Witness—Changing World*, Grand Rapids & Cambridge: Eerdmans Publishing, 1999, 193.

36 Mary Lou Codman-Wilson, 'Witness in the Midst of Religious Plurality: The Model of E. Stanley Jones' in Craig Van Gelder (ed.) *Confident Witness—Changing World*, Grand Rapids & Cambridge: Eerdmans Publishing, 1999, 203.

37 'A Movement of Hope for India: The Story of Sunil Sardar and Truthseekers International' by Barry Rodriguez, Whitney Vance and Erika Vance, New Delhi: Truthseekers, n.d., 10.

contextualized message of the Gospel to India's lower caste peoples (OBCs, Shudras) in ways they can better understand. Today millions of OBCs are seeking a way out of casteism.. Following in the footsteps of Mahatma Phule, Sunil's ministry has taken a stand for the rights of the poor through activism, representation and prayer. Braj Ranjan Mani explains that Phule utilized the legend of Bali for understanding India's history and the struggle 'for a democratic, casteless and inclusive society', and also employed the image of Bali to recall 'the Christian vision of a coming Redeemer, and the Judea-Christian paradigm of all human history as the working out of a battle between good and evil'.[38]

The bold mission of the Truthseekers movement is to end the caste system, not merely to lessen its negative effects, but to dismantle the caste system and 'all the societal pressures it creates'.[39] Truthseekers has a three-fold approach: 1) the Message of Jesus Christ who calls all people to equality and justice; 2) the Method is to build relationships between various caste leaders in order to create understanding; and 3) the Model is Foot Washing events where lowered-caste people have their feet washed by people of a higher caste or status in order to display a tangible contradiction to the caste system.[40]

For many in North India, Sunil Sardar has become an icon, a symbol of hope in their struggle for human dignity and justice for all. This too is an integral part of the vision of World Christianity in India today.

---

38 Braj Ranjan Mani, 'Truth behind the Myth of Bali and Vaman' in *The Balijan Cultural Movement Manifesto*, New Delhi: Balijan Cultural Movement, n.d., 15-16.

39 'A Movement of Hope for India: The Story of Sunil Sardar and Truthseekers International' by Barry Rodriguez, Whitney Vance and Erika Vance, New Delhi: Truthseekers, 5.

40 Ibid., 6.

Chapter 15

# In Conclusion and Continuation

India has an important role to fill in leadership and theological development of World Christianity. According to Walls, the shape and quality of World Christianity depends upon African and Asian theological scholarship.[1] Authentic theological scholarship must arise from the contexts and practice of Christian mission in Africa and Asia. 'If Africa, Asia, and Latin America do not develop a proper capacity for leadership in theological studies, there will be, for practical purposes, no theological studies anywhere that will be worth caring about'.[2] Africans perceive that the Western theological academy is sick, hence a call to reorient the theological academy to Christian mission, to put God back into theological studies. Western theological training shows little or no awareness of present world realities. 'Christianity's claim to universality' is demonstrated by its ability to inhabit and transform new cultures through fresh incarnations of the Savior, who

1 J. Kwabena Asamoah-Gyadu, '"Turning That Which Is Already There Toward Christ": The Contribution of Andrew F. Walls to Understanding African Christianity' in *Understanding World Christianity: The Vision and Work of Andrew F. Walls* edited by William R. Burrows, Mark R. Gornik, and Janice A. McLean, Maryknoll: Orbis Books, 2011, 208.

2 Ibid., 209.

'grows through the work of mission'.[3] Without a radical reorientation, seminarians and future church leaders 'are in danger of becoming theologically illiterate'.[4] This warning was from an Asian theologian who calls for fresh initiatives in documentation and development of new instruments for archival preservation and research.

## Archival Preservation and Documentation

In India there exists a great need for preservation and documentation of archival resources utilizing digital and other available techniques to rescue valuable documents, minutes, records and correspondence from destruction. 'Source documents are indispensable.... So new *repositories* and libraries need to be established, and new *instruments* need to be developed, to gather the hard evidence of Christianity around the world'.[5] The Centre for New Religious Movements at Birmingham, UK, is suggested as an example of the kind of infrastructure needed for continuing research in World Christianity.[6] Over the years India has seen the launching of a number of centres for various specialized fields of research. Some began well, then declined or failed for lack of interest or qualified leaders. Others thrive. A starting point will be to identify competent research scholars who can be trained as specialists in the developing new field of World Christianity Studies. A further need is for networking between interested scholars and existing institutions across denominational and confessional lines to form relationships and links with other Asian, African and Latino leaders and movers as well as with Western pioneers and potential partnership sources. Through it all a sense

---

3 Andrew Walls, cited by Gillian Bediako, 'Gospel and Culture: Andrew F. Walls in Africa, Africa in Andrew F. Walls' in *Understanding World Christianity: The Vision and Work of Andrew F. Walls* edited by William R. Burrows, Mark R. Gornik, and Janice A. McLean, Maryknoll: Orbis Books, 2011, 218.

4 Michael Poon, 'Andrew F. Walls and Documenting World Christianity in the Twenty-First Century' in *Understanding World Christianity: The Vision and Work of Andrew F. Walls* edited by William R. Burrows, Mark R. Gornik, and Janice A. McLean, Maryknoll: Orbis Books, 2011, 191.

5 Ibid., 178.

6 Ibid., 183.

of collegiality and collaboration for a common cause is needed, not the self-seeking aggrandizement and competition that is all too common.

## Asian & Indian Publications

Studies during the twentieth century of the African Independent Churches (AICs, also known as African Instituted or African Initiated Churches) are particularly valuable and have provided a background for the new World Christianity proposition by Andrew Walls and Lamin Sanneh. Asia has had fewer such studies of indigenous Christian movements and has much more yet to do. But a start has been made. Consider the following: *Christianity Made in Japan: A Study of Indigenous Movements* by Mark R. Mullins;[7] *Iglesia Ni Cristo: A Study in Independent Church Dynamics* by Leonard Tuggy;[8] *Christian Movements in Southeast Asia: A Theological Exploration* edited by Michael Nai-Chiu Poon;[9] *Fields of the Lord: Animism, Christian Minorities, and State Development in Indonesia* by Lorraine V. Aragon;[10] *The Liberating Gospel in China: The Christian Faith among China's Minority Peoples* by Ralph R. Covell;[11] *Jesus in Beijing: How Christianity is Transforming China and Changing the Global Balance of Power* by David Aikman;[12] *Asian and Pentecostal: The Charismatic Face of Christianity in Asia* edited by Allan Anderson

---

7 Mark R. Mullins, *Christianity Made in Japan: A Study of Indigenous Movements*, Honolulu: University of Hawai'i Press, 1998.

8 A. L. Tuggy, *Iglesia Ni Cristo: A Study in Independent Church Dynamics*, Quezon City, Philippines, 1976.

9 Michael Nai-Chiu Poon, ed., *Christian Movements in Southeast Asia: A Theological Exploration*, Singapore: Armour Publishing and Trinity Theological College, 2010.

10 Lorraine V. Aragon, *Fields of the Lord: Animism, Christian Minorities, and State Development in Indonesia*, Honolulu: University of Hawai'i Press, 2000.

11 Ralph R. Covell, *The Liberating Gospel in China: The Christian Faith among China's Minority Peoples*, Grand Rapids: Baker Books, 1995.

12 David Aikman, *Jesus in Beijing: How Christianity is Transforming China and Changing the Global Balance of Power*, Washington, D.C.: Regnery Publishing, 2003.

and Edmond Tang;[13] *The New Evangelicalism: Freeing the Church from Western Cultural Captivity* by Soong-Chan Rah;[14] *The Future of Evangelical Theology: Soundings from the Asian American Diaspora* by Amos Yong,[15] and others.

India as well has contributed several studies of importance. Among them: *Pioneers of Indigenous Christianity* by Kaj Baago;[16] also by Kaj Baago, *The Movement Around Subba Rao*;[17] *Roberto de Nobili on Indian Customs* by S. Rajamanickam;[18] *Jesus Christ and the Hindu Community: Is a Synthesis of Hinduism and Christianity Possible?* by Hans Staffner;[19] *Village Christians and Hindu Culture* by P. Y. Luke and John B. Carman;[20] 'Subaltern Movements and Indian Churches of Indigenous Origins' by Roger E. Hedlund;[21] *Quest for Identity, India's Churches of Indigenous Origin: The 'Little Tradition' in Indian Christianity* by Roger E. Hedlund;[22] *Christianity Is Indian: The Emergence of an Indigenous Community* edited by Roger E.

---

13 Allan Anderson and Edmond Tang, eds., *Asian and Pentecostal: The Charismatic Face of Christianity in Asia*, Oxford: Regnum Books, and Baguio City: APTS Press, 2005.

14 Soong-Chan Rah, *The New Evangelicalism: Freeing the Church from Western Cultural Captivity*, Downers Grove: InterVarsity Press, 2009.

15 Amos Yong, *The Future of Evangelical Theology: Soundings from the Asian American Diaspora*, Inter Varsity Press, Downers Grove, IL, 2014.

16 Kaj Baago, *Pioneers of Indigenous Christianity*, Madras: CLS, 1969.

17 Kaj Baago, *The Movement Around Subba Rao*, Madras: CLS, and Bangalore: CISRS, 1968.

18 S. Rajamanickam, *Roberto de Nobili on Indian Customs*, Palayamkottai: De Nobili Research Institute, St. Xavier's College, 1989.

19 Hans Staffner, *Jesus Christ and the Hindu Community: Is a Synthesis of Hinduism and Christianity Possible?* Anand: Gujarat Sahitya Prakash, 1988.

20 P. Y. Luke and John B. Carman, *Village Christians and Hindu Culture*, London: Lutterworth Press, and New York: Friendship Press, 1968.

21 Roger E. Hedlund, 'Subaltern Movements and Indian Churches of Indigenous Origins', *Journal of Dharma* XXII,1 (1998), 8-38.

22 Roger E. Hedlund, *Quest for Identity,India's Churches of Indigenous Origin: The 'Little Tradition' in Indian Christianity*, Delhi: ISPCK, and Chennai: MIIS, 2000.

Hedlund;[23] *Dalits and Christianity: Subaltern Religion and Liberation Theology in India* by Sathianathan Clarke;[24] *Dalits in India: Religion as a Source of Bondage or Liberation with Special Reference to Christians* by James Massey;[25] *The Indian Christians of St. Thomas* by Leslie Brown;[26] *India and the Latin Captivity of the Church* by R. H. S. Boyd;[27] 'Changing Perceptions of Indian Christians in Independent India' by Lionel Fernandes;[28] 'Abdul Masih: Icon of Indian Indigeneity' by Graham Kings;[29] 'Unbaptized Disciples of Christ?' by Julian Saldanha;[30] *Keshub Chunder Sen* by David C. Scott;[31] *A Christian Folk Religion in India: A Study of the Small Church Movement in Andhra Pradesh, with a Special Reference to the Bible Mission of Devadas* by P. Solomon Raj;[32] 'The History and Teachings of the Hindu Christian Community Commonly Called *Nattu Sabai* in Tirunelveli' by M. Thomas Thangaraj;[33] *I Follow*

23 Roger E. Hedlund, ed., *Christianity Is Indian: The Emergence of an Indigenous Community*, Revised, Delhi: ISPCK, and Chennai: MIIS, 2004.

24 Sathianathan Clarke, *Dalits and Christianity: Subaltern Religion and Liberation Theology in India*, New Delhi: Oxford University Press, 1998.

25 James Massey, *Dalits in India: Religion As a Source of Bondage or Liberation with Special Reference to Christians*, Delhi: Manohar Publications, 1995.

26 Leslie Brown, *The Indian Christians of St. Thomas*, Cambridge: The University Press, 1956, Madras: B.I Publications, 1990 reprint.

27 R. H. S. Boyd, *India and the Latin Captivity of the Church*, London: Cambridge University Press, 1974.

28 Lionel Fernandes, 'Changing Perceptions of Indian Christians in Independent India', *Jnanadeepa: Pune Journal of Religious Studies* Vol. 2, No. 2 (July 1999), 149-163.

29 Graham Kings, 'Abdul Masih: Icon of Indian Indigeneity', *International Bulletin of Missionary Research*, 23, 2 (April 1999), 66-69.

30 Julian Saldanha, 'Unbaptized Disciples of Christ'? *Third Millennium* I, 3 (July-September 1999), 20-27.

31 David C. Scott, *Keshub Chunder Sen*, Madras: CLS, 1979.

32 P. Solomon Raj, *A Christian Folk Religion in India: A Study of the Small Church Movement in Andhra Pradesh, with a Special Reference to the Bible Mission of Devadas*, Frankfurt: Peter Lang, 1986.

33 M. Thomas Thangaraj, 'The History and Teachings of the Hindu Christian Community Commonly Called *Nattu Sabai* in Tirunelveli', *Indian Church*

*After: An Autobiography* by Lakshmibai Tilak;[34] 'The Missionary Society of St. Thomas the Apostle: Its Beginnings' by S. Vadakel;[35] *K.E. Abraham: An Apostle from Modern India* by Habel G. Verghese;[36] *Narayan Vaman Tilak: The Christian Poet of Maharashtra* by J. C. Winslow;[37] 'Christianity in Hindu Polytheistic Structural Mould: Converts in Southern Tamilnadu Respond to an Alien Religion During "the Vasco da Gama Epoch"' by Felix Wilfred;[38] *Heralds of the Gospel in Asia* by Sebastian Karotemprel;[39] *A Biographical History of the Church in Nepal* by Cindy Perry;[40] *Ecclesial Identities in a Multi-Faith Context: Jesus Truth-Gatherings (Yeshu Satsangs) among Hindus and Sikhs in Northwest India* by Darren Todd Duerksen;[41] *Planting in Native Soil: Studies in Gospel Inculturation* edited by David Zersen and B. S. Moses Kumar;[42] as well as others.

---

*History Review*, Vol. V, No.1 (June 1971), 43-68;

34 Lakshmibai Tilak, *I Follow After: An Autobiography*, Translated by E. Josephine Inkster, Delhi: Oxford University Press, classic reissue, 1998.

35 S. Vadakel, 'The Missionary Society of St. Thomas the Apostle: Its Beginnings', *Indian Missiological Review* Vol. 20, No. 1 (March 1998), 28-37.

36 Habel G. Verghese, *K.E. Abraham: An Apostle from Modern India*, Kakambanad, Kerala: Christian Literature Service of India, 1974.

37 J.C. Winslow, *Narayan Vaman Tilak: The Christian Poet of Maharashtra*, Third edition, Pune: Word of Life Publications, 1996.

38 Felix Wilfred, 'Christianity in Hindu Polytheistic Structural Mould: Converts in Southern Tamilnadu Respond to an Alien Religion during "the Vasco da Gama Epoch",' *Archives de Sciences Sociales des Religions* 1998, 103 (Jullet-Septembre), 67-86.

39 Sebastian Karotemprel, *Heralds of the Gospel in Asia: A Study on Missionary Institutions in Asia*, Shillong: FABC Office of Evangelization, Sacred Heart Theological College, 1998.

40 Cindy Perry, *A Biographical History of the Church in Nepal*, Wheaton: Wheaton Graduate School, 1989.

41 Darren Todd Duerksen, *Ecclesial Identities in a Multi-Faith Context: Jesus Truth-Gatherings (Yeshu Satsangs) among Hindus and Sikhs in Northwest India*, Eugene, OR: Pickwick Publications, 2015.

42 David Zersen and B. S. Moses Kumar (eds.), *Planting in Native Soil: Studies in Gospel Inculturation*, Austin, Texas: Concordia University Press, and Delhi, India: ISPCK, 2014.

For readers desiring a more systematic coverage of Indian Christian history Robert Eric Frykenberg's *Christianity in India: From Beginnings to the Present* (New York: Oxford University Press, 2008) is recommended. Available volumes in the History of Christianity in India series published by the Church History Association of India also are highly recommended. These include: Vol. 1, *From the Beginning up to the Middle of the Sixteenth Century* by A. Mathias Mundadan (1984); Vol. 2, *From the Middle of the Sixteenth Century to the End of the Seventeenth Century* by Joseph Thekkedath (1982); Vol. 3, *During the Eighteenth Century* by E. R. Hambye (1997); Vol. 4, Part 2, *Tamilnadu in the Nineteenth and Twentieth Centuries* by Hugald Grafé (1990); Vol.5, Part 5, *North East India in the Nineteenth and Twentieth Centures* by Frederick S. Downs (1992).[43] Research scholars as well as others will be interested in the *Indian Church History Review* published twice a year by the Church History Association of India.[44]

Christianity belongs in India, if for no less a reason than its ancient apostolic roots in the well-attested Thomas tradition. In the pages of this introductory study we have endeavoured to catch glimpses of some of the highlights of Indian Christianity. Much more can yet be told. For additional information sources, readers are directed to the bibliographical references for further reading found at the end of this introductory account.

43 The History of Christianity in India series is published by the Church History Association of India, Bangalore, with several volumes still to be completed.

44 Inquiries should be directed to the Business Manager, Church History Association of India, C/o Dharmaram College, Hosur Road, Bangalore 560 029, India, or to the Executive Editor, Dr. Leonard Fernando, SJ, *Indian Church History Review,* C/o Vidya Jyoti, 23 Raj Niwas Marg, Delhi 110 054, India.

# Bibliography


Aghamkar, Atul Y. and Vishwas Padole, *Christian Missions in Maharashtra: Retrospect and Prospect,* Bangalore, TETRAWPOI, 2010.

Amaladass, Anand, "Dialogue between Hindus and the St. Thomas Christians" in *Hindu-Christian Dialogue: Perspectives and Encounters,* edited by Harold Coward, Delhi: Motilal Banarsidass Publishers, 1993.

Amaladass, Anand, "Indian Image of Christ" in *Co-worker for Your Joy: Festschrift in Honour of George Gispert-Sauch S.J.*, edited by S. Painadath and Leonard Fernando, Delhi: Vidyajyoti College and ISPCK, 2006.

Amaladass, Anand, *Jesuit Presence in Indian History: Commemorative Volume on the Occasion of the 150th Anniversary of the New Madurai Mission,1838-1988*, Anand, India: Gujarat Sahitya Prakash, 1988.

Anderson, Allan, "'The Present World-Wide Revival… Brought Up in India': Pandita Ramabai and the Origins of Pentecostalism" in *Indian and Christian: The Life and Legacy of Pandita Ramabai,* edited by Roger E. Hedlund, Sebastian KIM and Rajkumar Boaz Johnson, ISPCK, Delhi; MIIS, Chennai, 2011.

Anderson, Gerald H., John Roxborogh, John M. Prior SVD, and Christoffer H. Grundmann, *Witness to World Christianity: The International Association for Mission Studies, 1972-2012,* New Haven, CT: OMSC Publications, 2012.

Bauman, Chad M., *Christian Identity and Dalit Religion in Hindu India, 1868-1947*, Studies in the History of Christian Missions Series, Grand Rapids/Cambridge: Eerdmans Publishing Co., 2008.

Bergunder, Michael, *The South Indian Pentecostal Movement in the Twentieth Century*, Studies in the History of Christian Missions Series, Grand Rapids/Cambridge: Eerdmans Publishing Co., 2008.

Boyd, Robin H. S. *Khristadvaita: A Theology for India.* Madras: Christian Literature Service, 1977.

Braaten, Carl E. *The Flaming Center: A Theology of the Christian Mission*. Philadephia: Fortress Press, 1977.

Brown, Judith M. and Robert Eric Frykenberg (eds.), *Christians, Cultural Interactions, and India's Religious Traditions*, Studies in the History of Christian Missions Series, Grand Rapids/Cambridge: Eerdmans Publishing, 2002.

Brown, Leslie, *The Indian Christians of St. Thomas*, Cambridge University Press, Cambridge & New York, 1982. [An Indian edition, for sale in India only, was published by Mr. K. V. Mathew by special arrangement with Cambridge University Press, available at St. Thomas Service & Community Centre, Greams Road, Chennai, India.]

Burrows, William R., Mark R. Gornik and Ganice A. McLean (eds.), *Understanding World Christianity: The Vision and Work of Andrew F. Walls*, Maryknoll, NY: Orbis Books, 2011.

Carman, John B. "Christian Interpretation of 'Hinduism': Between Understanding and Theological Judgment" in *India and the Indianness of Christianity: Essays on Understanding–Historical, Theological, and Bibliographical–in Honor of Robert Eric Frykenberg*, edited by Richard Fox Young, Eerdmans Publishing, Grand Rapids Cambridge, 2009.

Chakravarti, Uma. *Rewriting History: The Life and Times of Pandita Ramabai*, New Delhi: Zubaan (Kali for Women), 2013 (1998).

Chan, Simon, *Grassroots Asian Theology: Thinking the Faith from the Ground Up*, Downers Grove, IL, InterVarsity Press, 2014.

Chatterjee, Sunil Kumar, "Pioneers of Indigeneity in Bengal" in *Christianity is Indian: The Emergence of an Indigenous Community*, edited by R. E. Hedlund, Delhi: ISPCK, Chennai: MIIS, revised 2004.

Clarke, Andrew D. and Bruce W. Winter (eds.) *One God, One Lord in a World of Religious Pluralism*. Cambridge: Tyndale House, 1991.

Correia-afonso, John (ed.) *Letters from the Mughal Court: The First Jesuit Mission to Akbar (1580-1583)*, Anand, India: Gujarat Sahitya Prakash, St. Louis, MO, USA: Institute of Jesuit Sources, 1981.

Coward, Harold (ed.), *Hindu-Christian Dialogue: Perspectives and Encounters*, Delhi: Motilal Banarsidass Publishers, 1993.

Dingrin, La Seng, "Conversion to Mission Christianity among the Kachin of Upper Burma, 1877-1972" in *Asia in the Making of Christianity: Conversion, Agency, and Indigeneity, 1600s to the Present,* edited by Richard Fox Young & Jonathan A. Seitz, Koninklijke Brill NV, Leiden/Boston, 2013.

Duerksen, Darren Todd, *Ecclesial Identities in a Multi-Faith Context: Jesus Truth-Gatherings (Yeshu Satsangs) among Hindus and Sikhs in Northwest India*, Eugene, OR: Pickwick Publications (Wipf & Stock), 2015.

Dupuis, Jacques. *Who Do You Say I Am? Introduction to Christology.* Maryknoll, NY: Orbis Books, 1994.

Ekka, Gabriel, "Catholic Church in Madhya Pradesh and Chhattisgarh" in the *Oxford Encyclopaedia of South Asian Christianity*, edited by R. E. Hedlund, J. M. Athyal, J. Kalapati and Jessica Richard, New Delhi: Oxford University Press, 2012.

Fernando, Leonard and G. Gispert-sauch, *Christianity in India: Two Thousand Years of Faith*, New Delhi: Viking Penguin, 2004.

Fox, Thomas C., *Pentecost in Asia: A New Way of Being Church*, Maryknoll, NY: Orbis Books, 2002.

Frenz, Matthias, "The Illusion of Conversion: Siva Meets Mary at Velankanni in Southern India" in *Asia in the Making of Christianity: Conversion, Agency, and Indigeneity, 1600s to the Present* edited by Richard Fox Young and Jonathan A. Seitz, Koninklijke Brill NV, Leiden/Boston, 2013.

Frykenberg, Robert Eric, *Christianity in India: From Beginnings to the Present*, New York: Oxford University Press, 2008.

Frykenberg, Robert Eric, "Pandita Ramabai and World Christianity" in *Indian and Christian: The Life and Legacy of Pandita Ramabai*, edited by Roger E. Hedlund, Sebastian KIM and Rajkumar Boaz Johnson, ISPCK, Delhi; MIIS, Chennai, 2011.

Frykenberg, Robert Eric (ed.), *Christians and Missionaries in India: Cross-Cultural Communication since 1500*, Studies in the History of Christian Missions Series, Grand Rapids/Cambridge: Eerdmans Publishing Co., 2003.

Gispert-sauch, George, "Xavier, Jerome (1549-1617)" in the *Oxford Encyclopaedia of South Asian Christianity*, edited by R. E. Hedlund, J. M. Athyal, J. Kalapati and Jessica Richard, New Delhi: Oxford University Press, 2012.

Gorospe, Adonis Abelard O. (ed.) *Naming the Unknown God*, Manila: Asian Theological Seminary and OMF Literature, 2006.

Greenman, Jeffrey and George Kalantzis (eds.), *Life in the Spirit: Spiritual Formation in Theological Perspective*, InterVarsity, Downers Grove, IL, USA, 2010.

Hedlund, Roger E., "Fourth Branch Christianity: Indigeneity, Contextuality, Pentecostalism, and Independent Christian Movements" in *A Cultured Faith: Essays in Honour of Prof. G. P. V. Somaratna on His Seventieth Birthday*, edited by Prabo Mihindukulasuriya, Ivor Poobalan and Ravin Caldera, Colombo, Sri Lanka: Colombo Theological Seminary, 2011.

Hedlund, Roger E., "Who Is Jesus?" Unit 1: Who is Jesus for Christians? Paper VI: The Person and Message of Jesus. M. A. Christian Studies by Correspondence, Department of Christian Studies, University of Madras, Chennai, 2003.

Hedlund, Roger E., *Quest for Identity: India's Churches of Indigenous Origin, The "Little Tradition" in Indian Christianity*, Delhi: ISPCK, Chennai: MIIS, 2000.

Hedlund, Roger E. (ed.), *Christianity is Indian: The Emergence of an Indigenous Community*, Delhi: ISPCK, Chennai: MIIS, revised 2004 (2000).

Hedlund, Roger E., Sebastian Kim and Rajkumar Boaz Johnson (eds.), *Indian and Christian: The Life and Legacy of Pandita Ramabai*, Delhi: ISPCK, Chennai: MIIS, 2011.

Hedlund, Roger E., J. M. Athyal, J. Kalapati and Jessica Richard (eds.), *Oxford Encyclopaedia of South Asian Christianity*, New Delhi: Oxford University Press, 2012.

James, Jonathan D., *McDonaldisation, Masala McGospel and Om Economics: Televangelism in Contemporary India*, New Delhi, Los Angeles, London and Singapore: SAGE Publications, 2010.

Jayakumar, Samuel, "Missionary Approach to Indigenous Culture: A Dalit Perspective" in *Christianity is Indian: The Emergence of an Indigenous Community*, edited by R. E. Hedlund, Delhi: ISPCK, Chennai: MIIS, revised 2004.

Jenkins, Philip, *The Lost History of Christianity: The Thousand-Year Golden Age of the Church in the Middle East, Africa, and Asia—and How it Died*, New York: HarperOne, 2008.

Jeyakumar, D. Arthur, *History of Christianity in India: Selected Themes*, Arasaradi, Madurai: Tamilnadu Theological Seminary, revised 2007.

Jeyaraj, Daniel, "Indian Participation in Enabling, Sustaining, and Promoting Christian Mission in India" in *India and the Indianness of Christianity: Essays on Understanding–Historical, Theological, and Bibliographical–in Honor of Robert Eric Frykenberg*, edited by Richard Fox Young, Eerdmans Publishing, Grand Rapids and Cambridge, 2009.

Jeyaraj, Daniel, "Mission Reports from South India and their Impact on the Western Mind: The Tranquebar Mission of the Eighteenth Century" in *Converting Colonialism: Visions and Realities in*

*Mission History, 1706-1914*, edited by Dana L. Robert, Grand Rapids/Cambridge: William B. Eerdmans Publishing Co., 2008.

Jones, E. Stanley, *Conversion*, New York/Nashville: Abingdon Press, 1959.

Kalapati, Joshua, *Dr. Radhakrishnan and Christianity: An Introduction to Hindu-Christian Apologetics*, Delhi: ISPCK, 2002.

Kalapati, Joshua and Ambrose Jeyasekaran T., *Life and Legacy of Madras Christian College, 1837-1978*, Chennai: Zha Communications, 2010.

Kalliath, Antony and Ernest W. Talibuddin (eds.), *Mission in Asia: Paths and Paradigms*, Pune: Fellowship of Indian Missiologists (FOIM), Bangalore: Asian Trading Corporation, 2011.

Keeley, Robin (ed.) *Eerdmans' Handbook to Christian Belief.* Grand Rapids: William B. Eerdmans Publishing Co., 1982.

Kim, Sebastian C. H., *In Search of Identity: Debates on Religious Conversion in India*, New Delhi: Oxford University Press, 2003.

Kim, Sebastian C. H. (ed.) *Christian Theology in Asia.* Cambridge: Cambridge University Press, 2008.

Koder, S. S., "Kerala and Her Jews", Cochin Synagogue, Mattancheri, Kerala, n.d.

Kumaradoss, Y. Vincent, *Robert Caldwell: A Scholar-Missionary in Colonial South India*, Delhi: ISPCK, 2008.

Lewis, Donald M. and Richard V. Pierard (eds.), *Global Evangelicalism: Theology, History and Culture in Regional Perspective*, Downers Grove: InterVarsity Press, 2014.

Lumsdaine, David H. (ed.), *Evangelical Christianity and Democracy in Asia*, Oxford and New York: Oxford University Press, 2009.

Maaker, Erik de, "Have the *Mitdes* Gone Silent? Conversion, Rhetoric, and the Continuing Importance of the Lower Deities in Northeast India" in *Asia in the Making of Christianity: Conversion, Agency, and Indigeneity, 1600s to the Present* edited by Richard Fox Young and Jonathan A. Seitz, Koninklijke Brill NV, Leiden/Boston, 2013.

Mallampalli, Chandra, "Caste, Catholicism, and History 'From Below', 1863-1917" in *India and the Indianness of Christianity: Essays on Understanding–Historical, Theological, and Bibliographical–in Honor of Robert Eric Frykenberg*, edited by Richard Fox Young, Eerdmans Publishing, Grand Rapids/ Cambridge, 2009.

Mattam, Joseph, "Xavier, Francis (1506-1552)" in the *Oxford Encyclopaedia of South Asian Christianity*, edited by R. E. Hedlund, J. M. Athyal, J. Kalapati and Jessica Richard, New Delhi: Oxford University Press, 2012.

Mihindukulasuriya, Prabo, Ivor Poobalan, and Ravin Caldera (eds.), *A Cultured Faith: Essays in honour of Prof. G. P. V. Somaratna on his Seventieth Birthday*, Kohuwela, Sri Lankaa: Colombo Theological Seminary, 2011.

Moffett, Samuel H., *A History of Christianity in Asia, Vol. 2: 1500-1900*, Orbis Books, Maryknoll, New York, USA, 2005.

Moreau, A. Scott (ed.), *Contextualization in World Missions: Mapping and Assessing Evangelical Models,* Kregel Academic, Grand Rapids, MI, USA, 2012.

Mukherjee, Sipra, "Conversion without 'Commotion': Rev. Lal Behari Day's *Candramukhir Upakhyan* (Story of Candramukhi)" in *Asia in the Making of Christianity: Conversion, Agency, and Indigeneity, 1600s to the Present*, edited by Richard Fox Young and Jonathan A. Seitz, Koninklijke Brill NV, Leiden/ Boston, 2013.

Neill, Stephen, *A History of Christianity in India: The Beginnings to AD 1707*, Cambridge: Cambridge University Press, 1984.

Neill, Stephen, *A History of Christianity in India: 1707-1858*, Cambridge: Cambridge University Press, 1985.

Newman, Henry S., *Days of Grace in India: A Record of Visits to Indian Missions*, London: S.W. Partridge & Co., Philadelphia: J.B. Lippincott & Co., Hoshangabad, India: Samuel Baker, ca 1880.

Noll, Mark A., *The New Shape of World Christianity: How American Experience Reflects Global Faith*, Downers Grove: InterVarsity Press, 2009.

Noll, Mark A. and Carolyn Nystrom, *Clouds of Witnesses: Christian Voices from Africa and Asia*, Downers Grove: InterVarsity Press, 2011.

Painadath, S. and Leonard Fernando (eds.), *Co-worker for Your Joy: Festschrift in honour of George Gispert-Sauch S.J.*, Delhi: Vidyajyoti College and ISPCK, 2006.

Pelikan, Jaroslav, *Jesus Through the Centuries: His Place in the History of Culture,* New Haven & London: Yale University Press, 1982.

Peskett, Howard and Vinoth Ramachandra, *The Message of Mission: The Glory of Christ in All Time and Space*. Delhi: ISPCK, and Chennai: MIIS, 2003.

Phan, Peter C. (ed.), *Christianities in Asia*, West Sussex, UK: Wiley-Blackwell Publishing, 2011.

Phan, Peter C. (ed.), *The Asian Synod: Texts and Commentaries*, Maryknoll, NY: Orbis Books, 2002.

Poon, Michael Nai-Chiu (ed.), *Christian Movements in Southeast Asia: A Theological Exploration*, Singapore: Trinity Theological College and Genesis Books, 2010.

Powell, Avril A., "Creating Christian Community in Early-Nineteenth-Century Agra" in *India and the Indianness of Christianity: Essays on Understanding–Historical, Theological, and Bibliographical–in Honor of Robert Eric Frykenberg*, edited by Richard Fox Young, Eerdmans Publishing, Grand Rapids/ Cambridge, 2009.

Powell, Mark Allan, *Jesus as a Figure in History: How Modern Historians View the Man from Galilee*, Louisville, Kentucky: Westminster John Knox Press, 1998.

Prakash, P. Surya, "Contributions of Sadhu Sundar Singh to the Indigenous Christian Movement in India" in *Christianity is Indian: The Emergence of an Indigenous Community*, edited by R. E. Hedlund, Delhi: ISPCK, Chennai: MIIS, revised 2004.

Raj, P. Peter, "Robert de Nobili: An Indigenous Foreigner" in *Christianity is Indian: The Emergence of an Indigenous Community* edited by R. E. Hedlund, Delhi: ISPCK, Chennai: MIIS, revised 2004.

Raj, Selva J. and Corinne G. Dempsey (eds.), *Popular Chritianity in India: Riting Between the Lines*, Albany: State University of New York Press, 2002.

Ramabai, Sarasvati, *Pandita Ramabai's America: Conditions of Life in the United States*, Edited with an Introduction by Robert Eric Frykenberg, Translated from Marathi by Kshitija Gomes, Philip C. Engblom, Translation Editor, Grand Rapids & Cambridge: Eerdmans Publishing, 2003.

Ramachandra, Vinoth, *Church and Mission in the New Asia: New Gods, New Identities,* with Responses from Simon Chan, Melba P. Maggay and Martin L. Sinaga, edited by Kimhong Hazra, Singapore: Trinity Theological College, 2009.

Rapaka, Yabbeju, "The Indian Pentecostal Church of God in Andhra Pradesh, 1932 to 2010: A Study of Dalit Pentecostalism," PhD Dissertation, School of Divinity, Regent University, Virginia Beach, USA, 2011.

Remban, Yuhanon, "Mission of the Malankara Orthodox Church" in the *Oxford Encyclopaedia of South Asian Christianity*, edited by R. E. Hedlund, J. M. Athyal, J. Kalapati and Jessica Richard, Oxford University Press, New Delhi, 2012.

Rethinasamy, E. Johnson, "Indigenous Christian Origins in Central Tamil Nadu" in *Christianity is Indian: The Emergence of an Indigenous Community*, edited by R. E. Hedlund, Delhi: ISPCK, Chennai: MIIS, revised 2004.

Richard, H. L., *Following Jesus in the Hindu Context: The Intriguing Implications of N. V. Tilak's Life and Thought*, William Carey Library, Pasadena, CA, 1998.

Robert, Dana L. *Christian Mission: How Christianity Became a World Religion*, Malden, MA, USA, and Oxford, UK: Wiley-Blackwell, 2009.

Robert, Dana L. (ed.), *Converting Colonialism: Visions and Realities in Mission History, 1706-1914*, Studies in the History of Christian

Missions Series, Grand Rapids/Cambridge: Eerdmans Publishing, 2008.

Sanneh, Lamin, *Disciples of All Nations: Pillars of World Christianity*, New York: Oxford University Press, 2008.

Sanneh, Lamin, *Translating the Message: The Missionary Impact on Culture*, Maryknoll, NY: Orbis Books, 1989.

Sanneh, Lamin, *Whose Religion is Christianity? The Gospel beyond the West*, Grand Rapids/Cambridge: Eerdmans Publishing, 2003.

Semple, Rhonda, "Connecting Disconnections: Troubling Meanings of Christian Conversion in Imperial North India" in *Asia in the Making of Christianity: Conversion, Agency, and Indigeneity, 1600s to the Present*, edited by Richard Fox Young and Jonathan A. Seitz, Koninklijke Brill NV, Leiden/ Boston, 2013.

Shaw, Mark, *Global Awakening: How 20th - Century Revivals Triggered a Christian Revolution*, Downers Grove: InterVarsity Press, 2010.

Snaitang, O. L. (ed.), *Churches of Indigenous Origins in Northeast India*, Delhi: ISPCK, Chennai: MIIS, 2000.

Solomon Raj, P., *The New Wine-skins: The Story of the Indigenous Missions in Coastal Andhra Pradesh, India*, Delhi: ISPCK, Chennai: MIIS, 2004.

Somaratna, G. P. V., *Origins of the Pentecostal Mission in Sri Lanka*, Nugegoda: Margaya Fellowship of Sri Lanka, 1996.

Tennent, Timothy C., *Building Christianity on Indian Foundations: The Legacy of Brahmabandhav Upadhyay*, Delhi: ISPCK, 2000.

Tennent, Timothy C., *Theology in the Context of World Christianity: How the Global Church is Influencing the Way we Think about and Discuss Theology*, Grand Rapids, MI: Zondervan, 2007.

Tete, Peter (ed.), *To Chotanagpur with Love and Service: Pioneers in the Ranchi Jesuit Province*, Ranchi: Ranchi Jesuit Society, 1991.

Thomas, Joy, "Christian Studies in Indian Universities" in the *Oxford Encyclopaedia of South Asian Christianity*, edited by R. E. Hedlund, J. M. Athyal, J. Kalapati and Jessica Richard, New Delhi: Oxford University Press, 2012.

Thomas, Joy, "Mission, Spirituality and Formation in Asia" in *Mission in Asia: Paths and Paradigms*, edited by Antony Kalliath CMI and Acharya Ernest W. Talibuddin, Fellowship of Indian Missiologists (FOIM), Ishvani Kendra, Pune, and Asian Trading Corporation, Bangalore, India, 2011.

Thomas, Pradip Ninan, *Strong Religion, Zealous Media: Christian Fundamentalism and Communication in India*, New Delhi, Los Angeles, London and Singapore: SAGE Publications, 2008.

Thonippara, Francis, "St. Thomas Christians: The First Indigenous Church of India" in *Christianity is Indian: The Emergence of an Indigenous Community*, edited by R. E. Hedlund, Delhi: ISPCK, Chennai: MIIS, revised 2004.

Venkatesh, K., "Living and Discipling in the Hindu World," *Mission Frontiers*, Bulletin of the U.S. Center for World Mission, Pasadena, May-June 2011, 16-17.

Visvanathan, Susan, *The Christians of Kerala: History, Belief and Ritual among the Yakoba,* New Delhi: Oxford University Press, 1993.

Walls, Andrew F., *The Missionary Movement in Christian History: Studies in the Transmission of Faith*, Maryknoll, NY: Orbis Books, Edinburgh: T&T Clark, 1996.

Walls, Andrew F.,*The Cross-Cultural Process in Christian History*, Maryknoll, NY: Orbis Books, and Edinburgh: T&T Clark, 2002.

Williams, C. Peter, "The Church Missionary Society and the Indigenous Church in the Second Half of the Nineteenth Century: The Defense and Destruction of the Venn Ideals" in *Converting Colonialism: Visions and Realities in Mission History, 1706-1914*, edited by Dana L. Robert, Grand Rapids/Cambridge: Eerdmans Publishing Co., 2008.

Woodberry, J. Dudley, "Contextualization among Muslims: Reusing Common Pillars" in *The Word among Us: Contextualizing Theology for Mission Today*, edited by Dean S. Gilliland, Word, Dallas, TX, USA, 1989.

Yong, Amos, *The Future of Evangelical Theology: Soundings from the Asian American Diaspora*, InterVarsity Press, Downers Grove, IL, 2014.

Young, Richard Fox, "Loss and Gain: An 'Intellectualist' Conversion and Its Socio-Cognitive Calculus in the Hindu-Christian Life of Nehemiah Goreh" in *Asia in the Making of Christianity: Conversion, Agency, and Indigeneity, 1600s to the Present*, edited by Richard Fox Young and Jonathan A. Seitz, Koninklijke Brill NV, Leiden/ Boston, 2013.

Young, Richard Fox (ed.), *India and the Indianness of Christianity: Essays on Understanding–Historical, Theological, and Bibliographical–in Honor of Robert Eric Frykenberg*, Studies in the History of Christian Missions Series, Grand Rapids and Cambridge: Eerdmans Publishing Co., 2009.

Young, Richard Fox and Jonathan A. Seitz (eds.), *Asia in the Making of Christianity: Conversion, Agency, and Indigeneity, 1600s to the Present*, Leiden and Boston: Brill, 2013.

Zersen, David and B. S. Moses Kumar (eds.), *Planting in Native Soil: Studies in Gospel Inculturation*, Concordia University Press, Austin, Texas USA, and ISPCK, Delhi, India, 2014.

# Index (Author/Subject)

## I



## J

## T

# Scriptures Quoted

*Exodus*
22:1

*Leviticus*
6:5
19:18

*Numbers*
5:7

*Isaiah*
61:1-2

*Matthew*
1:21
5-7
18:1
20:20-28
20:26
22:39

*Luke*
4:18-21
18:22
18:23-25
18:27
19:1-10
19:8
19:10